In the Scheme of Things

T0119886

In the Scheme of Things

Alternative Thinking on
the Practice of Architecture

Thomas R. Fisher

UNIVERSITY OF MINNESOTA PRESS

MINNEAPOLIS • LONDON

The University of Minnesota Press gratefully acknowledges the assistance provided for the publication of this book by the McKnight Foundation.

Copyright 2000 by Thomas R. Fisher

All rights reserved. No part of this publication may be reproduced, stored in a retrieval system, or transmitted, in any form or by any means, electronic, mechanical, photocopying, recording, or otherwise, without the prior written permission of the publisher.

Published by the University of Minnesota Press
111 Third Avenue South, Suite 290, Minneapolis, MN 55401–2520
http://www.upress.umn.edu

Developed and edited by Engine Books, Inc., New York
Interior book design by Gigantic Inc., New York

Printed in the United States of America on acid-free paper

LIBRARY OF CONGRESS CATALOGING-IN-PUBLICATION DATA

Fisher, Thomas, 1953–
   In the scheme of things : alternative thinking on the practice of architecture / Thomas R. Fisher.
     p. cm.
   The chapters originated as lectures or unpublished journal articles.
   Includes index.
   ISBN 0-8166-3653-2 (hc.) — ISBN 0-8166-3654-0 (pbk.)
     1. Architecture—Philosophy. 2. Architecture and society—History—20th Century. I. Title.
   NA2500 .F56 2000
   720'.1—dc21   99-089286

The University of Minnesota is an equal-opportunity educator and employer.

11 10 09 08 07 06   10 9 8 7 6 5 4 3 2 1

To Claudia, Ann, and Ellen

Contents

Acknowledgments

The chapters in this book all began as lectures or unpublished journal articles sponsored by both universities and professional associations, and I am grateful for the opportunity and support they gave me. They include the University of Minnesota, the Weisman Art Museum, AIA Minnesota, the *Harvard Architecture Journal*, the University of Toronto, the University of Wisconsin, Iowa State University, AIA Wisconsin, the University of Cincinnati, and AIA New York. I also want to thank my fellow editors at *Progressive Architecture* and my colleagues and students at the University of Minnesota for stimulating many of the ideas explored in these pieces. Those formerly or currently with both institutions have also had much to do with shaping this book. Ziva Freiman and Abby Bussel, both former editors at *Progressive Architecture*, have, along with their partner at Engine Books, Micaela Porta, done a terrific job editing the manuscript and steering it through to completion. At the same time, Julie Yee, *P/A*'s last art director, has applied her sure and subtle sense of graphics to the design of the book. Thanks, too, go to Douglas Armato, William Murphy, and Pieter Martin of the University of Minnesota Press for their generous support and encouragement of this project. Finally, I want to thank my family, my wife, Claudia, and my two daughters, Ann and Ellen, for their patience over the years as I have been on the road lecturing and at my desk writing. I hope that they—and you, the reader—find the book worthwhile.

Design in a World of **Flows**

We are in the midst of a tremendous social and economic transformation, as sweeping in its impact as the Industrial Revolution was some 150 to 200 years ago. The current process of change has been called many things: the global economy, the information revolution, the age of complexity. Whatever we call it, this break with the past has shaken the foundations of our economic and social lives, laid during the Industrial Revolution, and it has rendered vulnerable the various structures so carefully built upon those foundations, including the structures of the professions and the universities.

This transformation has been described by several thinkers as a series of shifts: from a mechanistic worldview view to one of organic flows; from an urge to dominate nature to one that seeks a balance with it; from mass production to mass customization; from large bureaucratic organizations to smaller project-based operations; from specialized jobs to versatility; and from professional autonomy to participatory teamwork.

A world of flows respects no boundaries. Investment capital flows around the globe to where it will produce the best return, ignoring efforts of policymakers to influence it. Information flows among people who have a need for it, despite efforts of governments to control it or publishers to charge for it. Work flows among companies and consultants to where it will achieve the most efficient production, without respect for location or nationality or community interests. People flow in and out of jobs that come and go with the merging, selling, diversifying, and downsizing of corporations, without much hope of ever achieving the security of their parents' generation.

Our socioeconomic world, in other words, is becoming more and more like the natural world, an ecology of myriad connections and flows that offers both great bounty and considerable hazard. The hazards, right now, are more apparent. As in the early, robber-baron stages of the Industrial Revolution, the information revolution has brought with it incredible hardship and inequity. The 350 richest individuals in the United States now hold almost as much wealth as the bottom 45 percent of the population. At the same time, people accustomed to having secure employment as long as they worked hard and their companies did well are finding that everyone's job is vulnerable, at the mercy of decisions made halfway across the country to please corporate boards and Wall Street investors.

This Darwinian struggle for the survival of the fittest has given rise to predators for whom the professions, as well as the weaker individuals among us, become prey. Consider the predatory practice of program managers who, like HMOs in the medical field, justify their pay by squeezing every dime of profit from architects' fees, or the opportunism of star designers who, in defiance of labor law, use unpaid employees or "consultant" staffs to compete against firms that play it fair. Look at the tactics being used in some quarters within the design professions, with firms undercutting each other to get work or with magazines assassinating their competitors to corner a market.

Behind much of this is a growing skepticism of professionalism. Professions are defined by the setting up of boundaries (the acquisition of an accredited degree or a professional license) that set the knowledge and skills of their members apart from the general public. However, in a world that elevates the marketplace, value is defined not by the degree or license one holds but by the effectiveness of what one does and the success of the results. Professionals who pay little attention to the needs of clients, or to the consequences of their decisions, become vulnerable. We see this in the hostility of some clients toward the design professions, as they turn to outside project managers, construction managers, and engineers to lead design teams, and to contractor-led or manufacturer-led design-build operations to implement the jobs.

The universities have traditionally been bulwarks against the most extreme aspects of the marketplace, but even here, survival of the fittest has begun to take hold on many campuses. Departments are increasingly valued according to the amount of outside money they bring in, and those euphemisms for cost cutting and layoffs—value engineering and reengineering—have begun to be applied to academic ranks. At the same time, the public and politicians have begun to demand more tangible, directly useful results from their investments in higher education, leading students to regard their time at school in strictly vocational terms and legislators and donors to weigh their allocations to schools using rather narrow cost-benefit analyses.

Not all is brutal in the global economic jungle, however. The breaking down of boundaries and the flowing together of things once thought distinct have also given rise to several innovations. Interdisciplinary work within universities, for example, has begun to blossom, with new areas of study, like critical theory, environmental studies, and ergonomics, arising out of the joint efforts of several traditional departments. Meanwhile, in the larger scheme of things, social mobility will increase and economic opportunities will abound for those who adapt to this new world, as occurred for those who adjusted to the Industrial Revolution.

It is easy to become pessimistic about the place of design and of the design professions in such a fast-paced, information-driven world, but I am very optimistic about the role both have to play. Indeed, I believe that design may have as central a place in a world of flows as science and technology had in the Industrial Revolution. In a world with little respect for traditional structures, almost everything—from the operation of a company to the organization of a community to the order of our physical environment—can be approached as a design problem, in which new solutions must be sought to meet particular needs and specific contexts.

The business world's notion of the virtual corporation as the ideal structure of companies in the information age is striking on two counts: not only do these virtual corporations mimic the traditional design firm in which people with various skills come together to work on a project and then disband, but each of these virtual companies also needs to redesign itself for each new venture, fitting its organization and operation to a particular project and context. Or consider the talk going on in many education departments about the benefits of project-based learning. Here too, the model they are following emulates that of the design studio, with teams of people learning through the solving of problems and the making of things. As in design, the lessons students learn in such a setting are interdisciplinary, integrative, and concrete.

Such examples of design thinking in other fields suggest that we must look at our own disciplines more broadly. One of the important transitions to be made by design schools over the next decade is to recast themselves as places where students learn to think critically as designers, while keeping the potential applications of that thinking as broad as possible. This is akin to the transition made in law schools earlier in this century, when students, formerly trained mainly in trial law, began to be encouraged to think like lawyers and to apply that thought process to everything from running a company to running a country. The design of buildings and landscapes will still be a major application of the knowledge generated in the design schools, but the design of organizations, operations, systems, codes, and policies of various sorts will become alternative routes for design graduates to take. That is where the market for our skills is growing most quickly and perhaps where the need for those skills is greatest. Consider that lawyers are now writing zoning codes, accountants determining housing policy, and engineers designing road and park systems, often badly.

The design professions need to become engaged in the entire life cycle of projects from the earliest determination of need and to encompass the processes of design and construction, maintenance, evolution, and repair. In some respects, landscape architects are much further in working this way than most architects, in part, I think, because of the tradition running from Patrick Geddes to Ian McHarg and beyond that looks holistically at regions and the interrelatedness of systems and their life cycles. Architects, driven by formal traditions that are more art-historical than ecological in origin, have let other groups—from program managers to construction managers to facilities managers—take responsibility for the life cycle of buildings. The design professions not only need to assume some of this responsibility, with the attendant financial and managerial skills it demands, but these management activities need to be welcomed into the design professions, much as the medical profession has embraced rather than fought such related groups as psychiatry and osteopathy.

There are signs of change. Some of the most successful large design firms have begun to offer clients a host of predesign services, such as strategic planning and marketing support, and they have moved aggressively into postdesign areas, such as facilities management and diagnostics. The small firms that are thriving have also carved out distinct niches within the full spectrum of services. A recent study of the architectural and legal professions has shown that the latter has done so well, in part, because lawyers do a much better job than architects in becoming long-term counselors to their clients and so spend much less time getting new work. The health of both architecture and landscape architecture depends upon our ability to become counselors to clients regarding their physical space needs, even when there is no major construction project on the horizon.

One way to do that is to become much more expansive in the types of teams we put together to solve clients' problems. I have heard of an architect joining forces with public health physicians to deliver more healthy indoor environments; of an architect allying with computer programmers to develop better virtual environments; and of landscape architects and archaeologists collaborating to reduce conflicts between historic resources and government-backed development. All such boundary-crossing efforts are positive steps that will help ensure the continued relevance of the design professions. The schools must find ways to prepare their graduates for a world that increasingly rewards those who can recruit and lead the most versatile teams, and those who are most entrepreneurial in the application of their knowledge.

How does this inform architectural practice and education? In reading the architectural literature in recent years, I've been struck by the dual desire on the part of both practitioners and educators to reflect the shifts occurring in our world on the one hand, and on the other to search for some sense of stability. Such a divergence is almost inherent in a world of flows. At a time when nothing seems stable and all things seem connected (an environment well suited to design thinking) there often occurs the counterweighing need for a place of belonging, where differences are accepted, as happens in a healthy community.

I believe that creating such a community demands a reconnection between practice and education, which have drifted apart in recent decades. Having a substantial number of practitioners teach, as some schools do, is one important way of integrating education and practice, and ways must be found to make practitioners feel like full members of the academic community. The schools also need to serve nonteaching practitioners, recognizing that they have a role to play in educating designers not just in their twenties but throughout their career. The continuing education requirement of the American Institute of Architects, for example, offers an opportunity for the schools to package educational programs for practitioners of all ages, which can either be held on campus or available electronically for study at home.

At the same time, practitioners have a wealth of experience and knowledge that the schools could help collect, organize, and disseminate to support the profession. The schools, for example, might invite practitioners to come and share with students specific lessons they have learned about design, technology, or practice matters, which would then be added to an electronic database available online to educators, alumni, and practitioners. Research done in the schools could also be published over an online system. Some practitioners might worry about giving away company secrets, but what we really should worry about is building the knowledge base and thus the value of our professions in a highly competitive world. The construction of such a knowledge base depends upon the cooperation of both practitioners and the schools.

Communicating what we do to the larger university and community constituencies is also a priority, and here the growing relevance of design can work to our advantage. There are what we would recognize as design discussions and debates going on in various departments: the design of structured programs in computer science; the design of complex systems in physics; the question of intelligent versus evolutionary design in biology. As with other transdisciplinary methods such as science, statistics, and logic, the design college could play the dual role of furthering specialized knowledge in its own disciplines as well as articulating general ways of thinking about design that are useful in other disciplines. Perhaps one way to begin such an effort would be to convene university-wide symposia in which members of various disciplines talk about their own design methods and design thinking.

Fostering links to other disciplines has practical as well as conceptual justification, as it helps secure the position of design schools within the university, despite their relatively meager research funding and endowments. The school of architecture at USC, for example, developed a series of design courses for nonmajors, which it promoted with the support of faculty and students and which helped take that school, in a matter of two years, from being deep in the red to well in the black. The outreach to nonmajors also has the benefit of beginning to educate our future clients, consultants, and constituencies about the value of design. During his tenure at Yale's school of architecture, Vincent Scully did much to benefit architects by virtue of the popular courses he taught to packed houses of nonmajors over the years, some number of whom became architectural clients.

The problem of defining the value of design is part of a larger debate about the value of knowledge work in our society, a discussion to which our disciplines have something to contribute. The biggest mistake corporations and universities make when "reengineering" is to see people as expenses that must be reduced as much as possible, much like the mistake some developers make when they see designers as the most expendable members of the building team. In an information age, the knowledge of people is the most important asset in any organization. By laying off experienced staff, companies throw away not only the investment they have made in training those people, but also the potential of experienced employees to avoid costly mistakes, find more efficient ways of doing things, and most of all, imagine new opportunities for applying their knowledge.

Designers, of course, excel at imagining better, more efficient, and more effective ways of doing things, and we know that central to the design process that others call "reengineering" is the ability to turn constraints into assets. But we have not done enough to communicate the relevance of design thinking to the problems of organizations. Nor have we adequately demonstrated the value that design brings to the physical environment. Design professionals talk a lot about improving the quality of life, but we rarely attempt to prove our case by returning to designed environments to document what worked, what didn't, and why. The failure to build such a critical and factual knowledge base has helped establish among some clients the misperception that designers add too little value to projects. Within the design disciplines, this lack of empirical knowledge has helped perpetuate an adolescent avant-garde that too often confuses the commission of errors with creative risk. We must be sure to take educated risks and eliminate avoidable errors, which demands that we work from knowledge rather than from the heroic lore that too often guides our actions.

In contributing to the flow of information and ideas within the universities and among professionals, the design schools can foster the connection of those two groups to the public at large. Like the professions, whose very licensure depends upon the demonstration of public benefit and the upholding of the public interest, the universities have a similar charge to increase the common good in exchange for public moneys. The design schools can be instrumental in demonstrating the commitment of both the professions and the universities to the public through various forms of activism. One model is the design school as the coordinator of university-wide interventions in the community. Some design schools, for example, have begun to involve faculty and students from architecture, planning, government, economics, and sociology who work as "SWAT teams" in troubled communities, helping them sort out problems and arrive at possible solutions. Another model is the idea of the teaching office that several schools have begun to experiment with. A few schools, for example, have begun placing students in architects' offices, working on pro bono community projects under the supervision of both faculty and practitioners, offering students real-world experience while attracting a lot of good press for both the school and the profession.

As these examples illustrate, much of the real excitement in our profession over the next decade lies in the structure of practice. I mean it very broadly: not just the structure of practicing architectural firms, but the structure of education, of interdisciplinary research, of community outreach. Any meaningful reform must go well beyond tinkering with practice support courses. The structure of practice is itself a design problem.

The reason the design community feels so embattled has more to do with our failure to recognize the power of our pedagogy than it does with the power of our competitors. I am very optimistic that we may reach our potential if we question the boundaries and structures and myths of our professional cultures that now limit our view of ourselves. A world of flows, profoundly ecological in nature if not in practice, favors those who have learned to see similar patterns among disparate things and underlying relationships among apparently unrelated functions. It favors, in other words, the designer.

Monocultures and **Multi**culturalism

The late Oxford historian Isaiah Berlin once characterized
the twentieth century as the one that tried to achieve
utopia and failed. When he made that comment, he was
referring to such utopian political ideas as communism and
fascism. But Isaiah Berlin could equally have been referring
to the fields of architecture, landscape architecture, and
urban design, for in this century we have tried, literally,
to build utopia, creating cities and suburbs based upon
utopian visions that for various reasons have failed us.
The question is, What lies ahead for us, in the wake of
a century of failed utopias? Do we simply give up on the
possibility of community and solidarity that prompted
our utopian thinking in the first place? Are we destined to
a future of atomistic individualism, a future of what Penn
State professor Christopher Clausen has called "post-
culturalism" in which "nothing is good or true unless it
satisfies me at this moment"? Or is it possible to achieve
a degree of cultural cohesion while still accommodating
cultural diversity? And if so, what role might the design
professions play in that creation?

These are questions particularly relevant to Americans. When Europeans began invading North America, they saw in it the possibility of a new society, in which human peace and solidarity could be attained. Many groups acted on that utopian urge, building settlements such as Zoar, Ohio, and New Harmony, Indiana, in which people acted collectively for the good of all. Although most of those utopian efforts eventually failed, they set out an ideal that became a defining character of this nation, the notion that we could achieve a unity among a plurality of people and cultures: *e pluribus unum*. And yet, creating a monoculture within a multicultural population has proven difficult.

Three utopian ideas have been particularly influential on what we have built in America in the twentieth century. The first is the rational utopia of René Descartes, the seventeenth-century French philosopher who, reacting to the "doubts and errors" of the scholastic education he received from the Jesuits, envisioned a world guided by reason and the certainty of mathematical order. The Cartesian utopia is one that seeks unity by imposing a geometric order on the perceived chaos of the world, seeking community through what we share as rational animals.

A second is the technological utopia of Francis Bacon, the seventeenth-century thinker who, frustrated by the backwardness of England in his time, foresaw a world driven by scientific discovery. Bacon held out the hope that we would achieve social unity through the common pursuit of technological advances and comforts, forging community out of our being tool-making animals.

The third is the organic utopia of Johann Gottfried von Herder, the eighteenth-century German writer who, rebelling against the Enlightenment views of his teacher, Immanuel Kant, envisioned a future in which different cultures would coexist, with each tied to the soil of a particular place. Herder's utopia attempted to formalize the apparent unity of vernacular culture, in which language and customs evolve over time, across generations.

These may seem like an odd group, but their ideas underpin the utopias that we have tried to build in this country over the past hundred years. Descartes's rational utopia, for example, is echoed in what has come to be known as the City Beautiful movement of the early twentieth century, led by architects such as Daniel Burnham. Burnham sought to impose a geometry of public spaces and a uniform facade of classical governmental architecture over the chaos of our rapidly growing industrial cities, which appealed to the Progressive Era belief that big government was a necessary counterweight to the rise of big business. Also implicit in the broad boulevards, ample parks, and great civic plazas of the City Beautiful movement was the classical ideal of the good life, which was to occur primarily in the public realm, with people behaving as rational beings engaged in self-governance. Here, then, was an architectural parallel to Descartes's idea that through the application of reason and the imposition of order, we can create a community amid the plurality of people and ideas.

To see the failings of that idea, we have only to look at where the City Beautiful movement led. Few of Burnham's city plans were ever fully realized, suggesting that the imposition of such a strict overall order is bound to remain incomplete in a liberal democracy such as ours. Likewise, the Roman classicism of the City Beautiful movement, as many scholars have noted, offered an imperialistic image at odds with the increasingly pluralistic population of our cities and the populism of Progressive Era politicians. Where this urbanism eventually found a home was among ruthless dictators, from Hitler's plans for Berlin as the capital of the Third Reich to Ceauşescu's plans for Bucharest in communist Romania.

The failure, then, of this Cartesian utopia is political in nature. Absent a dictator to make it happen, public space in this country is only rarely the coherent and pedestrian-oriented place of public gatherings and civic debates envisioned by Burnham. Instead, it has become largely a series of circulation routes for private transport moving us among private property. And if we have achieved Descartes's dream of rational order, it largely exists in the private realm, within our buildings and yards, rather than in our public space, which we increasingly view as a disordered and dangerous place.

Bacon's utopia of science and technology has had a more lasting effect on America's cities. The plans of Swiss architect Le Corbusier for Paris and German architect Ludwig Hilberseimer for a "Skyscraper city" exemplify Bacon's vision in *The New Atlantis* of a city of "high towers, the highest about half a mile in height," sustained by the fruits of modern technology. The ideal cities of Le Corbusier and Hilberseimer, with their rows of glass-clad towers set among highways, plazas, and parks, have, of course, become the model of corporate headquarters in downtown America and so hardly seem utopian to us anymore.

But it is utopian, when you consider that Le Corbusier and Hilberseimer meant their cities of towers as places to live as well as work. They seemed to see the uniformity of their towers as a neutral frame in which to accommodate a diverse population, similar to the neutrality that Bacon admired about science and technology. In all but the densest cities, however, living in towers has become largely the province of the poor or the rich. The poor often have little choice in the matter when it comes to publicly subsidized high-rise housing. The rich, however, have a choice. The increasingly common scenario of people being linked to global culture through media and electronics while the city outside decays, reveals the flaw in Bacon's utopia. He thought that a sense of community would arise through our common pursuit of technology, but the effect of technology has been to isolate us, to enable us to withdraw from one another.

Herder's utopia, the third we have tried to build in this century, has become perhaps the most common of all. He argued that diverse cultures arise out of their geographical circumstances and that various cultures should respect each other, but also maintain a distance with each remaining close to the land that gave it birth. Frank Lloyd Wright's Broadacre City has come close to this ideal in the twentieth century. Designed in the 1930s, it arose out of Wright's belief that American culture was inseparable from the American landscape, and that the strength of the American character derived from its connection to the land. Accordingly, Wright proposed in Broadacre City to give every house a piece of land to tend, going so far as to present a petition to Congress, signed by the likes of John Dewey and Albert Einstein, urging it to enact this vision into law. It needed no such legislation, however, because the marketplace took the idea of every house on its own acre and created suburbia.

So successful has this been that more people now live in the suburbs than in the cities or the country. But the suburbs have failed on one score: achieving Herder's utopian idea that if we stay rooted to the land, we will maintain a unified culture. Instead, so many of our suburbs have become places where we elevate personal consumption over community cohesion, and where we prize security over solidarity with people other than ourselves.

In the wake of utopian ideas that have enchanted us since the seventeenth century and that we have failed to achieve, how do we proceed? Many in the design professions have simply given up trying to build utopia, tending, as Voltaire put it, their own garden. And yet we cannot ignore the drive, so central to Western culture, to seek improvements in our condition based on an ideal.

Confronted by such a dilemma, the architectural community seems to have entered a time in which we pursue scaled-down utopias, a diversity of unities rather than a singular unified diversity. This may stem, in part, from the nature of design. Although many architects in the twentieth century were enamored with the idea of building singular utopias, design is inherently a particular activity, a matter of responding to the needs of particular people and to the demands of a particular site. Indeed, it may be that we were never able to build utopia because such particulars thankfully got in the way.

But what does it mean to create a diversity of unities? If traditional utopian thought has pursued unity, upon what basis might we now pursue diversity? One answer, I think, lies in ecology. We tend to think of ecology as applying to the natural world more than to the built world, more a matter of science than design. I believe that the dichotomy between design and ecology is a false one, and that ecological thinking can help us understand good design, and give us guidance to what a postutopian future might be like.

Take, for instance, the idea of monocultures. At the heart of most utopian thought lies the ideal of a human monoculture, of diverse people forming into a single, cohesive group. Ecologists, however, have demonstrated the limits of monocultures in the natural world, from which there is much that we might learn in building communities of people.

Consider a field of corn, with plants all of the same age and species. That agricultural monoculture clearly lends itself to harvesting in bulk, with the profits that go along with it, but, as ecologists have shown, that monoculture is dependent on machinery and chemicals and more vulnerable to disease and natural disasters such as drought or storms, than is a more diverse ecosystem. Much the same holds true for built monocultures, such as a housing development with units of the same age and size. Such housing is easier to construct than, say, scattered site housing of various types and sizes, and it offers its developers a more assured profit and a more focused pool of customers to market to. But like the urban monocultures of public housing, these developments have a greater vulnerability to economic disturbance.

During the housing boom and bust in New England in the 1990s, I watched an upscale condominium development across the street sell about one-third of the units at the initial offering of around $240,000, before the recession hit. After sitting on the mostly empty project for several years, the developer put the remaining units up for bid, with most selling for around $75,000. Because the units were essentially alike, all were subsequently assessed uniformly at the lowest price, causing the units that sold initially to lose about two-thirds of their value. That monoculture, in other words, was more vulnerable to devaluation than the more diverse housing stock in the immediate neighborhood, which did not lend itself to a lump assessment.

An example of what happens when a neighborhood sustains large and repeated economic disturbances is the inner city ghetto. As William Julius Wilson has documented in his book *When Work Disappears*, in the 1980s and 1990s America's ghettos experienced a severe and ongoing loss of jobs, to the point that once thriving and diverse communities became urban wildernesses where the survival of the fittest prevailed. From this perspective, an urban ghetto and a suburban tract development are economic monocultures that, appearances aside, differ mainly in the extent and duration of the disturbance they have faced.

An ecological view offers more than a critique of the mono-cultural communities we are now constructing. It also suggests various ways in which we might achieve the diversity that has so often eluded us in what we build. Ecologists describe three types of diversity in ecosystems, each of which is relevant to how we might design buildings and communities. The first type is alpha diversity, which measures the variety of species within a limited area. A tropical forest, for example, has a high alpha diversity, with many different kinds of plants and animals in each square mile, while a northern conifer forest, with few animal species and one predominant species of tree, has low alpha diversity.

An urban parallel to that might be the "new urbanism" of architects such as Duany Plater-Zyberk or the "fluid urbanism" of designers such as Michael Sorkin. Those two visions of our urban future are often viewed as opposed, since their forms are so different:

the one echoing the Cartesian city with its radial boulevards, terminus points, and street grids, while the other envisions a post-Cartesian world of nonlinear patterns, non-Euclidean forms, and ad hoc juxtapositions. Designers, however, frequently mistake differences of form for differences of substance, in this instance because these urban visions have an important commonality. Both propose communities in which diversity might flourish, either through the various sizes of housing in the one or the accommodation of variation in the other.

The notion of alpha diversity points to a limitation in what has been proposed so far by either camp. The geometries of both new urbanism and fluid urbanism, however different they might be, impose an overall order or design that seems antithetical to the evolved alpha diversity of an ecosystem, with various species pursuing their own patterns of life. This, in turn, suggests that as long as we pursue an overall "design" to a community that is conceived as a single property, an identifiable development, we are liable to design out the possibility of diversity, which must go beyond the size of houses or variety of forms. Ecology teaches us that diversity evolves, and it would seem that if we are to encourage more diverse communities, we must find ways in which they can evolve in small increments of property with a minimum of overall design.

That is not easily achieved, given the economies of scale and thus the financial return possible with the development of large tracts of land. Nor does the design community help when we disguise the monocultures created with superficial variations in style or form. One way of achieving a true alpha diversity in our cities involves the setting of growth boundaries at the rural edge, such as those established in places like Portland, Oregon, or Minneapolis and St. Paul, Minnesota. These restrictions on sprawl are forcing development to "infill" the many holes in the existing urban fabric. Another step entails the strengthening of preservation incentives to reuse existing structures, which reduces waste and enhances the temporal diversity of our cities and similarly dictates development on a smaller scale.

Ecologists describe another type—beta diversity—that exists not within a single ecosystem but between one ecosystem and another. A tropical rain forest, which has roughly the same species diversity uniformly distributed, has low beta diversity, while a northern temperate forest, with wetlands, areas of agriculture, and stands of both deciduous and coniferous trees, has relatively higher beta diversity. Each ecosystem might not be diverse in itself, but it varies greatly from those around it.

The significance of beta diversity is that it suggests a way in which we might achieve variety in an economy that favors mono-cultures. A region with agricultural monocultures can still have the sustainability and resistance to disturbance if mixed with enough "stands" of other species. The same might be said of an urban region. It might contain a number of monocultural housing developments targeting specific socioeconomic groups, but as long as the populations among the developments vary considerably and as long as the scale of and distance among the monocultures remain relatively small, a degree of diversity might be achieved.

Unfortunately, the scale and distance among monocultures in our cities are getting larger. Most new suburban communities vie for the most upscale housing to maximize tax revenues for the same amount of infrastructure, and most developers want to build for the same upscale population to maximize their profit for roughly the same amount of labor. And the distance between the suburban edge and inner city grows both psychologically and physically. Meanwhile, regional government, which might bridge between the inner city and suburban monocultures, exists for the most part in name only, and rarely has the political power to effect the kind of interdependence that a healthy, diverse ecosystem requires.

Design can help make these connections across human ecosystems. Some designers have shown how transit corridors and waterways, once used to separate neighborhoods, can generate civic or recreational space that allows ethnically and economically diverse groups of people to come together. Others have demonstrated the potential of "brownfield" sites, left vacant as industry abandoned our cities, for development that stitches together communities once divided by rail lines and factories. Even volunteer efforts, such as Habitat for Humanity, play a role, joining people of diverse backgrounds in a common cause. Physical space has been used in our cities for much of this century to keep people apart, and we still have much to learn in creating space that does just the opposite. Simply relocating a space or renaming it as public is not enough. The space of diversity must recognize and accommodate the different needs and expectations of people from various cultures, while providing ways in which they can find common ground.

A third type of diversity that obtains in the natural environment is temporal diversity. This is the tendency of a monoculture to become more diverse over time, unless resources and energy are put into maintaining its original character. One reason agricultural monocultures are less sustainable is the fact that they depend upon technology—chemicals, machinery, organized labor—to maintain their purity, as is also the case with urban monocultures. The amount and expense of technology—automotive and infrastructural—needed to maintain life in distant suburban developments are obvious. Perhaps less apparent is the tendency of older suburbs and older urban neighborhoods to become more diverse ethnically, economically, and physically over time.

In older suburbs, for example, active civic associations tend to spring up in response to what residents often see as evidence of decline. But if too successful, such civic associations can end up working against their own best interest. The increase in diversity in older neighborhoods makes them more sustainable over the long run and able, on average, to survive downturns in the economy better than communities in which a particular socioeconomic group prevails.

Architects, landscape architects, and urban designers are sometimes called in to help turn back the clock, to paper over change with design clichés like "antique" streetscape improvements or to hold back change with prescriptive design review ordinances to maintain the appearance of cohesion. The more difficult role for designers to play is as guides to change, providing advice on how to accommodate the needs and tastes of an increasingly diverse population while retaining some sense of the place as a whole. Temporal diversity also suggests that we sometimes undertake the hardest thing: not to do much of anything at all, to counsel against too much interference, and rather to use design to reveal the value of what is already there.

The search for such diverse unities may have little of the drama of the more reductive utopias that we have tried to build in this century. Nor does the designer's role as a physical ecologist have as much glamour as that associated with the great form-givers of the past hundred years, architects such as Daniel Burnham, Le Corbusier, and Frank Lloyd Wright. But what alternative do we have? In the wake of our failed utopias, we are facing a country still dominated by development in which, as the philosopher Jacques Derrida has argued, the very meaning of community is in danger of being lost. Multiculturalism as we now seem to practice it—at the scale of a solitary individual—is no culture at all. The only alternative I see involves creating conditions in which monocultural communities can evolve toward greater diversity, an objective that suggests a more modest role for the designer, and yet one that is broader, more visionary, and in the end more sustainable than that of the utopian.

Like most architects, I believe that what we do is valuable to our clients and to society at large. Probably, most of us believe that what we do is also value-laden, reflective of our own values as well as those of our clients and the larger community. But we have not been good at converting others to these beliefs; we have not been as effective as we should be in proving the value of what we do or in articulating the values implicit in our work. And yet, I can think of nothing more important for the profession right now.

Our inability to prove our value or articulate our values has a lot to do with the increasing marginalization of the profession within the building process, as competing service providers—program managers, construction managers, project managers—push the architect further and further away from the client, and delay the architect's input to ever more belated stages of the design process. These managers are hardly more skilled or more knowledgeable than we are. They simply have been much better at convincing clients of their value and, not insignificantly, convincing clients of our relative lack of value. They have not only told their story; we have allowed them to tell our story, to our detriment.

A growing number of engineers and interior designers have been able to convince clients that they can produce a functional building or interior as well as an architect can, and that they can come closer to meeting the client's budget and schedule. At the same time, a growing number of program managers have been able to convince clients that they can put together a project team and manage the building process more effectively than an architect, justifying their fees by squeezing those of everyone else.

There is plenty of evidence to the contrary. An engineer or design-builder, perhaps with an architecturally trained person somewhere in the back room, may indeed produce a functional building, but rarely one that provides far more than what was required of it in the program, as good design should. A program manager may be able to deliver a project on time and in budget, but rarely without eliminating through the cost-cutting measures of "value engineering" some of the very things that added value in the first place, such as long-term durability.

Knowing the real limits of these other players in the process won't get us very far if the client has come to believe their version of our value or if the client does not understand the values inherent in what architects do. Nor will we get very far if we play into the caricature others make of us: living up to our unfair reputation as expensive aesthetes with no sense of time or money management, or, according to one developer, as engineers with an attitude.

The Value and Values of Architecture

There are several reasons why we have played into our competitors' hands. First, we have tended to deemphasize written and verbal communication, having perhaps put too much trust in our drawing and modeling skills to convey our meaning, knowing full well that many clients have difficulty reading drawings or understanding the ideas in a model.

Admittedly, we also have tended to underestimate the importance of a working understanding of economics and finance, and of non-architectural skills such as time management. The schools have been partly to blame for this, mistakenly thinking that such things are vocational and thus beyond their responsibility. In doing so the schools have ignored the fact that these subjects are themselves areas of intellectual inquiry with methods related in some respects to those of design. But the blame goes beyond the schools; my first "all-nighter" was not at school but in a summer job at a firm that consistently ran behind schedule and over budget. The firm no longer exists.

A second, and possibly deeper, reason for some of our current troubles stems from the way many of us think about ourselves. In reaction to the perhaps overly rational quality of Modern architecture, we have, since the late 1960s, engaged in a kind of romantic rebellion that we call postmodernism, in which design has been seen as a personal exploration, a signature of each individual architect. Whatever else that has allowed, it has made it nearly impossible to analyze design or attempt to prove its value, since any such efforts are regarded by confirmed romantics as a threat to the mystery of our art, as if art and analysis are mutually exclusive.

A third and related difficulty also arises from this romantic rebellion. Most of us were taught in school to think of ourselves as individualists and even encouraged to be iconoclasts. One result of that individualism is that it has accustomed us to think of ourselves as competitors, something more characteristic of a trade than a profession. (Professions, for example, share information and build a common knowledge base; trades keep secrets.) This, in turn, leads to a self-destructive cycle in which the more embattled we become in the marketplace, the more competitive we become for the work still available, the less collegial we are in our conduct, and the more difficult it is to work together to address our value, not as individual firms but as a profession.

Another result of our cultivation of iconoclastic individualism is that we have difficulty articulating our values or relating them to those of the larger society. There is, to be sure, a certain critical perspective gained by such alienation from the larger culture, leading to the call in the avant-garde for a "critical architecture" or a "critical practice." Alienation, however, is problematic in this, the most social of the arts. I would argue that the greatest architecture of the past ennobled its culture rather than shunned it. Our responsibility as professionals is not to do "our own thing," but to do the right thing, to assert the common good over personal gain or expression, to represent the values to which we aspire as a culture.

To remain silent about the values represented in what we do, either out of mistaken belief that professionals must remain ethically neutral or out of a romantic dismissal of all normative values, is to eliminate one of the main reasons for the profession's very existence.

The Value and Values of Architecture

Many of our competitors can draw, build, and manage buildings. The architect has a somewhat different charge: making sure that what gets built not only meets the needs of the client, but of the larger public good—of the people who will use the building, members of the community who will look at it and visit it, and future generations who will have to maintain it. In that light, the difficulty we have in demonstrating our value is tied to the larger problem of our economy's unwillingness or inability to put a value on a building user's happiness, a community's aesthetic pleasure, or the accommodation of future generations. Our value is tied to protecting something that economists, at least, do not put a price upon. And yet the public itself still very much values such things, evident in the rise of design review boards, preservation commissions, and the like. While many architects sit on such committees, these entities have been assembled, in part, to protect communities against the inappropriate or self-serving projects that have characterized the work of too many architects.

I saw this cycle at work in the architectural magazines, whose current troubles reflect those of the profession. Compared to other fields, such as law and medicine, our profession has not exerted the same control over or provided the same support for our journals. We largely depend upon commercial publishers, as opposed to nonprofit or academic presses, to supply our major publications, which has enabled us to pay considerably less for annual subscriptions and to receive relatively higher quality printing and photo reproduction than what other professions enjoy. We have paid a price, though, for this bargain. The architectural magazines have had to pay as much attention to what sells as to what needs to be said or known. Those two motives are not mutually exclusive, and several of the architectural magazines have managed to do both well at different points in their lives. However, the architectural press in general has stood out among professional publishing in its focus on the most celebrated practitioners, on the most idiosyncratic projects, and on the most current fashions. Measured against journals in other fields, ours have devoted relatively little attention to common practices, typical problems, or broadly applicable solutions, and, as a result, we have had a rather poor record in building the sort of knowledge base that other professions have constructed and maintained with great care.

However dire our situation may seem, I remain hopeful because I believe that the public remains open to being convinced of our value. Our profession, like all the major professions, was founded on the idea of our looking after the public good, and I think the public wants us to do that. We, in turn, need to do at least two things.

First, we need to find a way, as a profession, to prove the added value of architectural services. That will demand going beyond a smattering of advertising and public relations based on broad and largely unsupported generalizations that design improves the quality of life. We must begin to document in a rigorous manner the consequences—good and bad—of what we do and to communicate those effects in a way that ordinary people understand. Done well, such an effort would begin to counter the perception among too many people that architecture is an expense to be minimized or that architects are aesthetes who must be managed. The documentation of the value we bring would also equip us with the tools we need to demonstrate that we can protect people's investment by making sure that it is spent in the most effective and creative way to meet the greatest number of needs in the most timely fashion.

Other fields offer us an example of how this might take place. Consider the brokerage profession. Its members are well paid and it has attracted a tremendous amount of both public and private investment, even with the knowledge that the investment may lose money. The stock market in the 1990s has reached record highs, in part because that profession has done a very good job of demonstrating that stock investments outperform all other kinds of investments over the long term, an argument that every broker makes and has ample evidence—available industrywide—to prove it. That united effort at proving the value of brokerage services has occurred in spite of the intense competition that exists among the various brokerage houses. Each individual firm set aside its differences for the good of the whole.

Of course, architecture is not like investing and buildings are not like stocks. Nevertheless a building, like an investment, performs. We can measure that performance in a variety of ways, be it in terms of assessed value or leasing rates or worker productivity or retail sales. The main difference between our field and that of brokerage is that brokers know not only how particular stocks have performed, but also how the industry as a whole has performed over time. Brokers can demonstrate that investing in the market is, in the long term, better than, say, putting one's money in a savings account or under the mattress. Architects have remarkably little knowledge of this kind. It is only now becoming a more common practice for architects to return to their buildings and rigorously assess what worked and what didn't. (During the last few years of *Progressive Architecture* magazine's existence, we began returning to buildings a year or two after completion and found a great deal of anger among clients and users. The resentments arose not so much from the fact that not everything worked perfectly, but that the architects had never returned to ask about the problems.) And we have almost no knowledge of how architect-designed buildings have performed in relation to those that are not—even though to a client with an increasing number of options for the delivery of a building, that may be the most pertinent information upon which to base a decision.

The reason clients could use that information brings us to another parallel between investing and architecture, one that we often don't face as squarely as stockbrokers do. That is the matter of risk. We tend to downplay risk, holding up our compliance with the building and zoning codes as evidence. Clients, however, are well aware of the risk in hiring an architect, not because there is a possibility of the building falling down but because the outcome of investing their money and time seems so unpredictable. As opposed to a prefabricated metal building, for instance, architecture involves an exploration, a process of discovering solutions to complex needs or tectonic problems. The result of such a process is unknown at the beginning, in the same sense that the outcome of a stock investment, even in the most blue chip of companies, is unpredictable.

The long-term record of stock performance minimizes the sense of exposure for investments. We do not possess such data, which may be why some clients, operating in a highly volatile economy, go to those who offer a more predictable result, such as an engineer or a turnkey design builder or a package interior designer-manufacturer.

But the brokerage industry has used risk to its advantage, showing how risk and return are related. Even neophyte investors are aware that the higher the risk, the higher the potential return on their investment.

We, too, should know what the return has been for architects who have taken relatively larger risks versus those who have not. The reason has to do with fees. Without this knowledge, everyone is competing based on the lowest fees, which makes it difficult to do any high-risk (exploratory, ground-breaking) architecture. In such a climate, too many architects are forced to do unimaginative "low-risk" work, and a few architects to do high-risk work for ridiculously low fees. Besides the need to know the return on high-risk work, we should know what kind of risks are worth taking and which aren't. This would enable us to charge fees based not on bidding or price cutting, but on the degree of return we historically have provided.

Building such a knowledge base may seem too daunting a task, but I believe it is possible and absolutely necessary if this profession is to thrive. It is possible because the means of accomplishing this are at hand, and the main obstacle has more to do with our own romantic self-image than it does with the allocation of time or money.

The process might go something like this: a representative group would establish a method by which firms begin collecting information about their own work, using certain agreed measures depending upon the building type, client type, and so on. Residential architects could collect information on assessed values of the houses they have designed and on how those assessments compare with the value of similar houses in the area. Commercial architects might compare the rental rates or leasing percentages of their buildings to similar buildings in which design played a minimal role. Industrial architects might examine the operation costs of their buildings or the productivity of employees and compare them to other mass-produced facilities. The profession, in other words, could become a frontline data collector. The common good would impel all firms to pool the information, anonymously if so desired, to begin to build a shared database.

The schools of architecture could help in instructing firms about basic data-gathering methods and could work with the American Institute of Architects to pursue funding to begin cataloging, organizing, and redistributing this information to every architect for use with clients. In that way, we can begin to create an information loop related to the value of architectural services, arming the profession with the kind of knowledge it needs to compete and providing appropriately supportive and essential roles for both the schools and the AIA.

There would be risks here, as there are with every research project. For example, not every architecturally designed building may perform substantially better than those delivered by other means, but all the more reason to find out where the real value of what we do lies, where the risks we take pay off and where they don't. There are also significant rewards for such a sustained effort in demonstrating our values as a profession. When I write about buildings and, in the process, talk to various people from the architect to the janitor, I am constantly struck by how often the discussion involves questions of values—what people want in their work or their home, how people see themselves and how their environment might reflect that, and how people interact with each other and what is required to make that interaction happen. I am likewise struck by how wide a gap sometimes exists between the values of building users and those of architects. The addressing of values is, I think, the very stuff of architecture, what sets it apart from mere building. But we cannot exclude from examination our own values as a profession, values that, particularly in the past fifty years, have tended to diverge from those of the people we design for. I don't mean to portray the architect as a social deviant. Most architects share in the aspirations of the larger culture: property ownership, familial security, community involvement, personal liberty and growth. But the architectural culture, like the arts culture generally, has set itself apart from the bourgeoisie on matters of taste in a tired refrain from the old Modernist avant-garde. We should not overreact to that tradition and, as some postmodernists have done, blindly accept popular taste and willfully pander to public prejudices. Rather, we should look critically at what we value, examining the assumptions, contradictions, and consequences of what we hold dear.

Building the architectural knowledge base thus entails not only quantifiable measures, but qualitative documentation of what people value. We may find that our values do not jibe, but understanding and to a degree empathizing with values one does not hold is central not only to architecture but to politics, both of which must find ways, organizationally and structurally, to bring people together. We can have all the information possible about the consequences of what we do, but we also need a better grasp of the political judgment necessary to apply that knowledge appropriately, at the right time in the right place. We call that design, but it also goes by the name of leadership, and there are few things in this world that people value more than that.

The Architect as a **Social Hieroglyphic**

After architecture school and a few years of work in an architectural office, I attended a graduate program in the humanities, where I spent long days sitting by the water in Annapolis, listening to the Navy cadets run through their drills while I read, with a certain relish, supposedly subversive books like Karl Marx's *Das Kapital*. I baffled some of my college friends when I entered that program. It seemed far removed from the profession of architecture, but I found almost all of it, including Marx, extremely relevant to the situations in which architects often find themselves.

Take Marx's discussion of commodities. "A commodity appears, at first sight, a very trivial thing, and easily understood," he wrote. "Its analysis shows that it is, in reality, a very queer thing, abounding in metaphysical subtleties and theoretical niceties." One such subtlety he saw is the way in which capitalistic societies develop a "fetishism" for people as well as products, turning them into a symbol or "social hieroglyphic" of some deeper aspect of ourselves and our social relations.

Architects have been both victors and victims of this commodity formation. We have certainly taken advantage of the commodification of building products, and we have paid a price for our success. In many offices, design now entails a process of assembling products out of catalogs. Many of these products are so consistent in performance and competitive in price that they have become commodities, a "hieroglyphic" of all the engineering that had gone into their making. Such products have increasingly become fetishized as well. When manufacturers start advertising urinals in "designer" colors or door-knobs silhouetted against a softly lighted backdrop, you know that you are in the presence of "a very queer thing," as Marx put it.

This has also diminished what we do. As building products have become more technically uniform, we find ourselves making product choices based on appearance, or taste, which places us in a vulnerable position in the public eye. When architects become consumers of commodities, it raises the obvious question of what expertise we bring to our selection. The public seems to exclude architects from making selections based on technical knowledge, in the manner of a physician's choice of medicines being based on a diagnosis, for example, or of a lawyer's argument being based on precedent.

Commodity formation has affected not just product selection, but architecture itself. Look at how our economy positions architecture. The quality of a work of architecture matters hardly at all in terms of its assessment or depreciation for tax purposes and has almost no bearing on its market value, which is usually based upon what similar structures in an area have sold for. Resale value, of course, can some-times be enhanced if a building is associated with a famous architect, but that is almost always a factor of the association rather than the value attached to the inherent qualities of the building itself. At the same time, a work of architecture that is unlike anything else and lacks the cachet of a famous name attached to it often has a lower market value. None of this is to say that architectural quality is unimportant. But it does show how much the process of commodifying buildings is, itself, resistant to the intangible or immeasurable aspects of architecture.

Architects, up to now, have generally been free of this process. A tax assessor or a real estate agent might be blind to matters of architectural quality, but that has typically not been the case with clients intent on commissioning an architectural firm for a project. All kinds of intangibles—how well the architects seem to listen to the client, how interested the architects appear to be in the job, how comfortable the client feels with the people who will work on the project, how much the client likes the firm's other work—have traditionally been important in the choosing of one firm over another.

Those factors still matter. However, architects in all parts of the country, in firms of all sizes and types, report the increasing frequency with which clients now make their selection based upon the lowest architectural fee or upon how many other projects a firm has done exactly like the one contemplated. This trend has accelerated regardless of economic conditions, during the construction booms of the 1980s and late 1990s as well as during the downturn in the early nineties. Representing the inroads that marketplace values have made in all of the professions, many architectural firms are viewed as interchangeable and thus are forced to compete based upon their fee or specialization.

The common response of firms has been to accept the demands of their commodification. Some firms have found ways to reduce overhead and the level of services in order to lower their fees. This, however, has proven extremely risky, since the courts continue to hold architects liable for work performed by consultants or other members of the project team. In other words, the title "architect" brings with it certain legal expectations that do not reflect the reduced services or limited role of architects on many jobs. Other firms have specialized in particular building types or even in specific components of buildings. But this, too, has its risks: a sudden downturn in construction activity in a firm's area of specialization can be devastating, as we have seen with developer-oriented firms in the late 1980s.

Still other firms have sought to avoid this commodification altogether through the care and feeding of their own reputations. Their assumption is that if a firm is well enough known—locally or internationally, for the quality of its design work or its service—it can remain immune to such things as fee bidding. In some cases that is true. The best-known architects, even though they, too, must now work hard to get commissions, generally seem to command adequate fees and to do a fairly wide range of work. But they have not escaped commodification of a different sort.

Among certain clients or within the architectural community, fetishes tend to develop around well-known architects' work: the press attends to almost everything they build, schools continually pursue them for lectures and exhibitions, and clients who care about architectural quality arrive at their doorstep. A twofold trap awaits such architects. There is considerable pressure put upon them to repeat, with some variation, the forms that propelled them to stardom in the first place, pushing many well-known architects to eventually become caricatures of their "former" selves. There also arises, with a name-brand architect's initial success, the temptation to expand or to accept an amount of work that lies beyond the firm's ability to control. Thus, even if the work of such architects doesn't become stale, it frequently becomes less consistent, less refined, or less thought-out. There have been noted exceptions to this fate, but it has demanded that the architects walk away from their own success and reinvent themselves and their work, as happened with the multiple careers of Frank Lloyd Wright. Very few noted architects have followed this path.

It may seem that architects are destined to become either interchangeable commodities or the object of fetishes. I do not think that is true. But there remains the legitimate question of why we should be concerned about the commodification of architects. You could argue that many architects have prospered in the process. Or you could say that it has benefited consumers. Fee bidding, for example, allows clients to get the best-priced service from architects, and specialization, the most foolproof service. You could claim that this process has strengthened the architectural profession by making it more competitive or more responsive to market demands.

There is an element of truth in such economic arguments, but what they overlook are the noneconomic consequences of commodification. Look at its effect on people: thousands of professionals were unemployed or underemployed in the mid-1990s, as the very developers who accelerated the commodification of the architect in the 1980s brought on a collapse of the market for architectural services. Or consider the effect of commodification on the built environment: since World War II, and especially in the past decade or two, construction has become more shoddy, the character of most buildings has become more banal, and the forms of high-style architecture have become ever more strident. There are many reasons for this. The rapid tax write-off of buildings, the declining skill level of many tradespeople, and the falling standard of living in this country have all contributed to the decreasing quality of construction. But the commodification of the architect has been a key factor.

As architects are increasingly pressured to lower fees below the level required for even a minimum of service, they are not given a chance to work out the details of a building or even to observe its construction to ensure that the details are properly handled in the field. No thorough-going survey has yet been done of buildings constructed in this manner, but I suspect you would find that a remarkable number are beset by major problems of one sort or another.

Likewise, the push toward specialization among architects has contributed to the banality of so many buildings: the house-plan shops that turn out superficial variations of the same few house types, the specialized hospital firms that seem to lose sight of architecture amid all of the functional requirements, or the commercial firms that mass-produce strip shopping centers or suburban office buildings or light industrial facilities. Some specialized firms do manage to break out of this mold and make architecture worthy of the name. For the most part, however, firms that specialize in a specific building type, particularly one controlled by developers, work in a system that effectively discourages good design.

And, for somewhat different reasons, the same systemic problem applies to many high-design firms. They, too, become specialists of a sort: specialists in their own signature style. As already noted, the very success of these firms and the desire of at least some clients to capitalize upon that success puts pressure on these architects to produce essentially the same kind of work, leading, in many cases, to an eventual decline in design quality.

Accepting the idea, then, that the commodification of architects has become a fact of professional life and that its physical consequences are less than desirable, what can be done to change the situation? Is there anything that a person or a firm can do to resist a force that is so pervasive and so much a part of a capitalistic economy such as ours? I think there is, although such resistance requires a fairly dramatic shift in the way architects typically think about themselves and their work.

Perhaps the best way to suggest alternatives is through example, and the practice of the late Charles and Ray Eames comes closest to what I have in mind. The Eameses are known within the architectural community mainly for their own house and a few other case-study houses that they designed. Their work has begun to interest a younger generation of designers, sick of the empty excesses of postmodernism, who see the Eameses' minimalist aesthetic, with its mix of technical rigor and intellectual richness, holding promise for our own time. But rather than their aesthetic, it is their practice that offers a still-viable model of how we might resist commodification.

Some may find that claim paradoxical. The Eameses, for example, were famous in their own time (the 1940s through the mid-1970s) and were often covered in both the popular and professional press. Also, much of their work involved the design and manufacture of products, or commodities, intended for sale. On the surface, at least, they would seem to be very much affected by the process of commodification. Yet even a cursory examination of their career shows how well they resisted the effects of this process—the fee bidding, specialization, or emphasis on a signature style.

The Eameses' view of design was absolutely crucial to this act of resistance. Design, for them, was a process, not the attribute of a product; it was an exploration to find the best way to "accomplish a particular purpose," as Charles Eames once said, rather than an activity aimed at resulting in an aesthetically pleasing object. The Eameses, of course, designed many such objects over the thirty-eight years that they ran their studio, producing everything from leg splints, airplane parts, furniture, and children's toys to films, magazine covers, exhibitions, and governmental reports. But rarely did they start out with the intention of making a particular object. Rather, the objects they made were the by-product of design explorations that had the potential to go in any number of directions. The Eameses began their studio in 1941 with the intention of studying the possibilities of molded plywood, not with the objectives of making leg splints or airplane wings.

They further resisted commodification by never allowing themselves to be associated with any particular type of work, set of forms, or established profession. The pressure on many ostensibly interchangeable firms to lower fees or to specialize was moot for them. Unlike any other firm, they were generalists working in a wide area. Likewise, the pressure on famous designers to repeat a signature style or characteristic set of shapes was obviated by the Eameses' disconnection of design from form making. It is impossible to commodify a process or predict the results of an open-ended exploration. Perhaps most important, the Eameses resisted commodification by never allying with any one discipline or profession. Charles Eames was trained as an architect and Ray Eames as a painter, but they worked not only as architects and artists but as graphic designers, furniture designers, interior designers, industrial designers, exhibit designers, filmmakers, engineers, manufacturers, scientists, and inventors.

You could argue that our economy can support only a very few generalists such as the Eameses or that they lived at a time when specialization within the professions was not as common as it is now. However, the Eameses themselves refuted such claims. They demonstrated, through the very success of their studio, that there is a demand for design, rightly considered, in a large number of fields and that there are many clients able to support such a generalist activity. Their criticism of specialization within the design professions, voiced as early as the 1940s, also shows that that trend is not new.

Rather than dismiss the Eameses as exceptions to the rule or ignore them, as has been the case in the past few decades, we should embrace their model as a way to avoid the commodification that most designers now face. To do so will require changes in two of our most powerful and conservative institutions: the universities and the professions. The Eameses' generalist, interdisciplinary approach to design, for example, runs against the closely guarded disciplinary boundaries and highly specialized divisions of knowledge within the modern university. Design, as conceived by the Eameses, would not be just another academic specialization, but taught as a methodology of problem solving, akin to logic or inductive reasoning, in every department. Designers would have a legitimate place, like historians and philosophers do, in every discipline.

Implicit in the Eameses' work is a critique of the design of the university itself. The modern university, with its roots in the Enlightenment, is an efficient mechanism for developing and transferring information, but it is not well-suited to addressing the complex, multifaceted problems of our times—crime, addiction, unemployment, discrimination, ethnic hatred, and so on. Were we to design a university in response to such needs, it almost certainly would have a more flexible, interdisciplinary structure, where students and professors from various fields could more readily work together in task-oriented teams.

A similar restructuring of the professions is implicit in the Eameses' interpretation of design. Like the universities, the professions play a valuable role in generating knowledge and transferring technical information. But every profession is limited to the extent that it is defined by its ends and not its means. Architects are licensed to design buildings, doctors to cure people, lawyers to lead people through the justice system. There is, accordingly, a real disincentive for professionals to produce results or even to recommend actions other than what they are licensed to do. Rare is the architect, for example, who, upon hearing a client's needs, would suggest that a building not be built or an existing structure not be upgraded in some way.

The Eameses' conception of design as an exploration with no predictable direction or outcome runs against the assumptions not only of the design community, but also of all professions. Indeed, their methods suggest a way in which the professions could be defined not according to what they produce, but to how they think. The designer, in other words, would be someone who works intuitively, structuring and then solving ill-defined problems; the doctor, someone who works comparatively, diagnosing malfunctions and applying cures based upon a search of the existing knowledge base; the lawyer, someone who works historically, looking to precedent to frame new interpretations.

Such institutional changes are not likely to happen soon, although they are probably necessary in the long run if our universities and the other professions are to avoid the commodification that has overtaken architects. As for the architectural profession, we must first acknowledge our own commodification before we can see our unique position in addressing it—as the very sort of complex, ill-defined problem designers are best at solving.

The **Fictions** of Architecture

For as long as I can remember, both buildings and books have fascinated me, both the physical spaces we enclose in steel and glass and the imagined spaces we create with words on a page. I grew up assuming a connection between the two—until college, at which point I realized that others did not assume such a connection at all. The faculty and students of architecture and literature rarely interacted and the two curricula allowed almost no crossover of courses and credits. The separation of the two disciplines became most clear to me in my third year, when an architecture professor cautioned me against taking time away from design studio to edit a campus magazine, as if, to paraphrase Victor Hugo, the book might kill the building.

If anything will kill the building, it is the "disconnect" between architecture and fiction. Although the two disciplines use different media and pursue different means of expression, architecture and fiction share a common, if often invisible, underpinning. They both involve similar actions, such as the making of marks on paper or the imagining of spaces we inhabit, and similar ways of thinking. I believe that the impoverishment of architecture and the marginalization of architects in recent decades stem, in part, from our failure as a profession to recognize what ordinary people often take for granted: that buildings reflect the fictions we create about the world.

Our disconnect from fiction is not entirely our fault. Literature has, in the past few decades, diverged quite markedly from the sort of fictions architects have traditionally engaged. As the writer Robert Shacochis has argued, literary fiction "has turned markedly inward... rejecting the macrocosm for the microcosm, exercising an imagination that never leaves home or, worse, never leaves the self." Recent architecture has not been immune from this self-involvement. Some of the most visible and talked-about architecture in our time has arisen from architects' private fictions, in which personal obsessions or idiosyncratic forms have largely driven the designs.

In general, though, architects have pursued what I will call public fictions, imaginative acts and symbolic gestures that embody the collective values and ideas of a community in a particular place and time. Architecture's public fictions are as diverse as the communities they speak to and the architects who work with them, but to use Shacochis's term, such fictions embrace the "macrocosm," the public realm, even when they result in buildings intended for private clients.

To some, the notion of a public fiction may sound like a contradiction in terms. There exists the widely held belief, perhaps explaining the inwardness of recent fictional writing, that the public realm has become so fragmented and public consensus so improbable that we should not even try to address them through art. That is a circular and self-fulfilling argument: the more we neglect the public realm, the more its decline justifies our neglect. No art, especially the very public art of architecture, can thrive if, as Shacochis says, it "never leaves home." Indeed, some of the current difficulties facing the architectural profession stem from our not recognizing and not defending the public fictions that we engage and which, in many ways, define us as a profession.

What, then, constitutes a public fiction in architecture? I have found the ideas of a late-nineteenth and early-twentieth-century German thinker, Hans Vaihinger, helpful here. His major book, a relatively obscure work entitled *The Philosophy of "As If,"* explains a lot about what we do as architects. Vaihinger thought that all creativity involves the making of fictions, which he called "hybrid and ambiguous thought structures used to attain a purpose indirectly." A fiction, in other words, involves acting "as if" something is true even when we know full well that it is not. Vaihinger made a clear distinction between a fiction and a hypothesis. A hypothesis is an idea that we hope to prove true. A fiction, in contrast, we know to be untrue, but, like a tool, it proves useful to us at the moment to clarify something or to help us see it in a new way.

Architects create such fictions all the time. When we talk about a building's plan having a circulation "spine" or having wings like "arms," or having a front-office "head" and a back-office "tail," we engage the sort of fictions Vaihinger wrote about. We design "as if" the parts of a building are like parts of the body in order to understand the building elements' roles or their effect on us. The fictional names and identities we give to aspects of buildings allow us to design more efficiently, to understand problems or resolutions more clearly, and to grasp ideas more strongly, so as not to lose them amid the competing forces and complex issues of architecture.

As in literature, some architectural fictions have more lasting power than others do. In most cases, an architectural fiction has a short life. It helps us see what we are doing on a project or helps us explain it to someone else, but once it has served its purpose, we put it back in our conceptual toolbox. Some architects, however, are more ambitious: beyond immediate, personal utility, their fictional ideas are meant to have long-term, public meaning. In such cases, the fiction often applies not just to an aspect of one building, but to an entire body of work, to the context in which the work occurs, and to the way in which we live and work. As great literature has always done, such architectural fictions reveal paradoxes at the core of every problem. We return time and again to some buildings, as to some books, to glimpse what is often most hidden from us and to try to resolve what are ultimately unresolvable questions. Buildings like these resonate with a broad spectrum of people, giving concrete expression to widely held values. Through such public fictions, architects construct and care for the public realm.

Let me give an example. Unlike the work of some Modern architects, that of Le Corbusier has generally withstood the barbs of postmodern critics because the fictions that underlie his architecture remain as relevant now as they were in the early twentieth century. I use fictions in the plural because, as many have observed, Le Corbusier seemed to change the guiding fiction behind his work midway through his career. In his early years in practice, he embraced the fiction of the machine, designing "as if" his buildings and the modern world in general had become one large mechanism: an efficient, integrated system of highways and high-rises, column grids and curtain walls.

This idea occurred in the work of many artists and writers of Le Corbusier's generation, but he pursued the fiction further than most architects did. For him, the power of the machine lay not in its superficial characteristics—its streamlined shapes and unornamented surfaces—but in its creation of *objets-types*, mass-manufactured products whose forms reflect functional requirements and material constraints distinct from the "dead concepts" of the past. His 1915 Maison Dom-Ino idea, for example, envisioned a building as an inter-related system of types—columns, floors, walls, stairs—stripped to the most elemental form that their function demanded and material allowed. It also served as a metaphor for what more and more people, at least in the West, had begun to experience: a work life increasingly affected by Frederick Taylor's gospel of efficiency; a home life transformed by home economics and domestic science; a mental life rid of its dark corners by Freudian psychoanalysis. Le Corbusier's House Machine became not just a solution to the design of buildings, but a metaphor for early-twentieth-century Western culture.

Like many great fictions, this one was not new. It recalled, among other works, that of the seventeenth-century writer Francis Bacon, whose 1627 book *The New Atlantis* envisioned a fictional island, complete with glass towers not unlike Le Corbusier's 1925 Plan Voisin for Paris, where people sought health and happiness through the pursuit of science and the application of technology. Le

Corbusier updated the story for a century actually capable of achieving what Bacon, three hundred years earlier, could only dream of.

Later in his life, though, Le Corbusier appears to make an about-face. In projects such as the Ronchamp Chapel, he pursues the fiction of a community living in nature in isolation from a corrupting culture. The project itself generated that fiction to a certain extent. "Given the existing conditions on top of an isolated hill," wrote Le Corbusier, "a single organized working group, a homogeneous team, a knowledgeable technique, men up there free and masters of their work," he designed a chapel whose thick curving walls, dark damp interior, sloped stone floor, and mysterious top lighting recall our first shelter: the cave.

The fiction of a harmonious life in nature is also an old story. The eighteenth-century thinker Jean-Jacques Rousseau argued most memorably that society corrupts us and that the "noble savage" living in a state of nature was the happiest and most free. An idea that has motivated virtually every romantic thinker since then, Rousseau's fiction may seem far removed from modernity's machine metaphor, evident in the criticism leveled at Le Corbusier's seemingly heretical change of mind in his late work. As architect James Stirling wrote in response to projects such as Ronchamp, "The flight from the 'academicism' of pre-war modern is questionable when it produces an architecture of the irrational."

But this misses the connection that Le Corbusier's work reveals between the fiction of the machine and that of the noble savage. Arising out of the rubble of World War II, the chapel at Ronchamp speaks to the primitivism at the heart of the modern age. The more powerful our technology, the more savage we had become in applying it. (Rousseau alluded to this when he wrote, "Nothing could be more unhappy than savage man, dazzled by science, tormented by his passions.") Indeed, Le Corbusier did not do an about-face so much as he shifted his emphasis. The fictions of nature and the machine, of the organic and the mechanistic, depend upon each other, like opposite sides of the same coin. We keep coming back to Le Corbusier's work in part because of the paradox at the center of modern life that it explores.

Le Corbusier also went beyond simply building these public fictions. Like that other great architectural fictionalist of our century, Frank Lloyd Wright, Le Corbusier brought his ideas before a broader audience through books, tours, press events, and the like. An element of self-promotion prompted such actions. Still, Le Corbusier, like Wright, emphasized his ideas about the public realm in most of this publicity, instigating debate about issues of public import, such as the role of technology in modern life, the relationship of the individual to a community, and so on.

Public fictions of various sorts inform the work of architects today, although like writers we have been generally less outspoken about them and less willing to engage in public discussion about them. Nevertheless, these fictions underpin our profession and remain central to the intellectual life of the discipline and to the public's valuing of what we do.

The fiction of the machine continues unabated in the work of architects such as Norman Foster. In his firm's Hong Kong Bank, for instance, the building operates as well as looks like a machine, with cranes that enable repairs, removable service units that allow updating, and moveable parts that respond to changes in function or climatic conditions. Flexibility and adaptability underlie this mechanistic fiction, and to a certain extent those qualities do exist in the building. But equally evident is the control exerted over the workplace, with everything down to the desk accessories detailed as part of an integrated, consistent system. While the remarkable uniformity of the furniture and fixtures may reflect Hong Kong's cultural context, in which personal expression in public is less tolerated than in the West, the bank also expresses the ironies of technological freedom. We gain freedom of movement, freedom to change within the confines of the system, but we also lose the freedom to act independently of that system or to individualize any part of it beyond what the design allows.

The paradox of "collective freedom" continues in the organization of Foster's practice. His staff works at long tables in a single room, with Foster among them. As projects move through the office, they also move along the table, from designers to detailers, in a kind of human assembly line. The process is not repetitive as an assembly line would be, yet it is rational and systematic, allowing for flexibility and rapid change, but little privacy or personalization. You could argue that such control is appropriate in the workplace. But like his buildings, Foster's office raises questions about the nature of freedom in the machine age. Such questions deserve debate, especially with respect to the public realm, in which, paradoxically, we have unprecedented freedom of movement, for example, via the automobile, even as we experience unprecedented restrictions on actions that are not part of the system, such as walking in an automobile-dominated landscape. We act as if technology liberates us, but only within the bounds determined by those who design the technology.

The work of Christopher Alexander in some sense inverts that paradox. His pattern language builds an entire repertoire of architectural elements—window seats, covered walks, and so on—based on desired human actions such as sitting by light or walking in the shade, which Alexander believes exist across cultures and across time. It is a universal system of individual actions, a technology of the personal. The machine, in contrast, plays a subordinate role in Alexander's work. In buildings such as the Julian Street Inn in San Jose, California, Alexander employs modern mass-produced materials such as concrete block and tile roofing, but the overall building has a handcrafted character, with sculpted and painted concrete walls, columns, and dining room trusses.

That, in turn, has affected Alexander's practice. He takes part in constructing his designs, working as an architect and a contractor, rejecting the separation that has grown between the two functions. Likewise, he designs by meeting the future inhabitant on the site and talking about where the building will go and what it should be like before he begins to draw, rejecting the notion of the architect as a white-collar office worker. Alexander is certainly systematic and consistent in applying his principles to all aspects of his architecture and his practice, but therein lies the paradox of this work. The fiction of individual difference, with its responsiveness to people's needs via the pattern language, is countered by the fiction of universal truths embedded in that language, which denies the cultural differences among people and the divergent needs that arise from those differences.

The fiction of the state of nature, of the organic community isolated from the corruptions of the modern world, has also seen new life since the time of Le Corbusier and Frank Lloyd Wright. In some cases, this has taken the form of a return to a previous time, a golden age considered more whole or more viable than our own period. The work of the architect Quinlan Terry offers one example. Viewing Modern architecture as a kind of aberration in the long history of Classical architecture in the West, Terry designs buildings that not only look as if they were designed before the nineteenth century, but that are also constructed that way, with solid masonry walls, wood windows, and slate roofs. He uses a Modern argument for his antimodern work. Classical architecture, he argues, is as functional, as accommodating of new problems, and as cost-effective as Modern architecture, and even more durable, given that most traditional building materials are "practically inert."

This fiction of a classical golden age carries over into the way in which Terry practices. He has an office in Dedham, England, and he and his staff produce drawings by hand in a style reminiscent of the Classical architects he admires, such as Palladio. The drawings typically mix elevations, plans, and occasional details on a single sheet, with an italic script—evoking a time in the seventeenth and eighteenth centuries when architects could, with relatively few drawings and scant specifications, entrust contractors with the construction of buildings based on the use of traditional materials and details. The paradox here is that this antimodern fiction still exists within a modern world in which many contractors have lost the knowledge of such traditions and in which owners' requirements do not neatly fit into

Classical forms. Terry's Howard Building at Cambridge offers an example, where the interior functions conflict with the exterior arrangement of windows, resulting in the blocking of several openings. While that in itself is not a critical flaw, it reveals the unresolvable contradiction of all fictions of a more holistic, more organic "golden age": they can neither bring back the past nor entirely block out the present, however they might have us imagine otherwise.

A very different form of this sort of fiction occurs in the architecture of William McDonough. The work of his firm looks to a time in the past when architecture was more sustainable, more respectful of and interactive with the natural environment. McDonough seeks this not by constructing buildings as they were hundreds of years ago, but by using the most advanced technology available to us to achieve an age-old goal. In buildings such as the Miller SQA office and manufacturing building in Holland, Michigan, the architects have used daylighting and ventilation techniques to increase the satisfaction of the people who work inside and to dramatically decrease the use of energy. In other projects, McDonough has made the manufacturing plants actually improve local environmental conditions with water, for example, leaving the facility cleaner than it was when it went in.

Here, too, the fiction of the building as an integral part of the natural environment carries over into the operation of McDonough's office. While he runs a fairly traditional architectural practice, he also has a business that employs chemists and engineers to develop more sustainable materials and processes for use in construction. McDonough has become a spokesperson on this issue, writing, teaching, lecturing, and appearing on television before a broad audience, as both Wright and Le Corbusier did in their own day. The fiction of a more sustainable past masks the fact that human cultures, even those supposedly in tune with their natural environment, have never been truly in balance with the natural world. The archaeological record offers ample evidence of traditional cultures that overgrazed and over-cultivated the land, or that depended upon and eventually depleted finite resources. Knowledge of that history does not deny the value of trying to achieve such a balance in the future, but it serves to remind us that sustainability is, in the end, a fiction that may never totally align with reality.

Problems arise when we are not clear about our fictions, falling into one of two traps that Vaihinger cautions us against in his philosophy of "as if." One trap occurs when we fail to distinguish between hypothesis and fiction. In a hypothesis we posit an idea capable of being shown to be true, while with a fiction we create ideas that may or may not be true, but which are useful in provoking thought, eliciting comment, clarifying an idea. Each has its place, but the architectural profession has conflated them many times, especially during the twentieth century. When Le Corbusier put forward his Plan Voisin for Paris, for example, with its vision of clearing the old city and replacing it with towers in a park, he created a fiction about the relationship of nature and culture, of technology and habitation, of past and future. It was meant to provoke debate, not to present a schematic design for the demolition of Paris. Yet those who took this fiction too literally, including Le Corbusier himself later in life, began to act upon this fiction as if it were meant to be implemented. And implemented it was, in the centers of cities worldwide, to the great detriment of urban life. If the public has become wary of architects, it is for just such a confusion of fiction and reality, where we must have seemed like mad scientists experimenting with whole populations in the process of testing our (fictional) ideas.

Vaihinger cautions us about another error, which has occurred more recently, in which fictions are allowed to stray so far from the facts that they no longer have any meaning. At one time, this may not have constituted much of a peril for architects. If our ideas ventured too far from reality, they would remain on paper and never be built. However, the rise of powerful computer simulations has encouraged, in some schools, the development of fictional environments in which gravity and function no longer obtain, all done in the name of architecture. As I have discovered, when questioning whether such things are architecture, however interesting they might be as computer explorations, one is likely to be called a philistine. Nevertheless, this does raise an important point about architecture as a public fiction. The public aspect of what we do is such that if we meander too far from the factual world, we undercut ourselves. We might invigorate another discipline, such as computer graphics, but we should not confuse this with the making of architecture.

If problems arise when we conflate fact and fiction, so, too, do we encounter difficulties when we overlook the fictional nature of what we do altogether. Large numbers of architecture firms do not see themselves involved in fictional thinking at all, but rather as simply delivering functional buildings that purportedly meet their clients' needs. This is the equivalent of writers who claim that their fictional worlds are entirely factual, something that no one believes and that, in the case of journalists, is cause for dismissal. The problem this creates for architects is that there are many other nonarchitects who can also deliver functional buildings, perhaps better and almost certainly cheaper than we can. The denial of our fictional role in society is, I think, behind the perception of the architect on the part of many clients as a commodity, whose fees can be endlessly squeezed and who may even be one of the most expendable members of the building team. Architecture, if it is to survive as a profession, must be about more than meeting the building code and keeping out the water. It must connect to people's deepest values and aspirations, their beliefs about the past and desires for the future—the very things that all great writers trade in.

At the other extreme, there are a few architects who employ highly personal, signature styles as a way of distinguishing themselves both in the marketplace and in the eyes of their colleagues. They are akin to the novelists who write only about themselves in a hermetic or highly personal manner. While the act of reading—a generally solitary activity—might accommodate such solipsism in written fiction, it is death to architecture. Ours is inherently a social art, a public art that is used and shared by many people. An architecture that is highly personal or idiosyncratic in nature not only lets the public down, but has the effect of trivializing the discipline. If architecture is only a matter of personal style, then one style becomes as good as another, one person's taste as good as another's. The irony here is that signature architects can become commodities of a different sort, trapped in the style that made them famous. Le Corbusier, as we saw, transformed himself midway through his career. No signature architects could survive doing the same today, so dependent have they become on the work that flows in because of their personal style.

As a profession, we need to change how we think of ourselves and how we present ourselves to the public. We must begin to address questions that matter to the public at large. Finding the questions that matter, of course, is not easy. Not only have the professions withdrawn from the public realm in recent decades, focusing more on internal, theoretical, or technical questions than on political or ethical ones, but so have many ordinary people retreated from public life, whether physically behind locked doors, barred windows, and gated communities, or socially behind the divisions of class and race.

This creates significant difficulty for architects, since the formation of the public realm is one of the core tasks of our discipline. As a profession we are often assailed on the grounds of our not knowing enough about construction, or our not taking enough responsibility for the building team, or our not competing forcefully enough against interlopers. But the question of our professional value rests, I believe, on a more fundamental problem: our having lost our social role as public storytellers and visionaries.

By that, I do not mean that we have no purpose. The design of functional, durable, appealing buildings remains an important task for all of us. But our public purpose goes beyond that to envisioning possible futures that people can believe in, be inspired by, and work toward. We possess the most powerful of methods, one that can make the most abstract idea or ephemeral ideal concrete and understandable. But we have backed away from making our fictions public and have, instead, followed the road of fiction writers in becoming more self-referential and self-involved.

We have precedent to guide us out of this corner. Many architects in the past have realized the importance of telling their fictions to the public. When Le Corbusier came forward with his Plan Voisin or when Wright created Broadacre City or announced his scheme for the mile-high skyscraper, they engaged in one of the central tasks of the architect, creating powerful fictions and telling them to the public in ways ordinary people could understand. Some, perhaps all of the visionary schemes just mentioned, may not have been what we would have wanted realized, but in some ways that did not matter. They were catalyzing ideas that focused public debate.

We need to take up that role again if we are ever to regain the confidence of the public upon which, after all, we are dependent to grant us the monopoly of architectural licensure. We must stop talking just to ourselves in a jargon that even we can no longer understand, and learn to communicate clearly and directly, as the best architects of the past have always done. We must stop seeing pro bono projects and visionary schemes and advocacy positions as extraneous activities, and begin to realize that they are at the very core of what it means to be an architect. And we must stop being embarrassed about the ideals of this profession, for the sake of appearing to be more practical or hardheaded. Thus we may start to recover our former place with the leaders of society, who are tellers of public fictions just like we are.

I grew up wanting to be like my grandfather, a Beaux-Arts-trained architect with a practice in Detroit. As a youth I admired not just the combination of creativity and command that went with being an architect, but the all-encompassing quality of the architectural culture, which affected my grandfather's behavior, his view of the world, even his clothing and demeanor. I do not remember him wearing anything other than a suit, even at family picnics or on casual walks. As I became a teenager, looking for ways to rebel, my grandfather's difference from the rest of the adults I knew made him and his line of work even more enticing. In college, however, facing the prospect of becoming an architect myself, I came to see a darker side to what I had so long aspired to. As with many architects, my grandfather's preoccupation with his work had created marital difficulties and familial discord. Also, as with many architects, my grandfather's insulation from the culture around him, which had been so appealing when I was younger, came to seem self-defeating, as it isolated him from the very people he had to design for. I began to realize that the design culture, epitomized by my grandfather, had become an obstacle to success as an architect.

That concern grew more pressing as I worked in architectural offices and then wrote about the profession. Time and again, I saw creative people hold back from responding to rapidly changing market conditions; the brightest even seemed to take pride in their perilous financial state and increasingly marginal role in the design and construction process. A similar malaise existed in academia—what might be summarized as a "disconnect" between design education and the rest of the university and society—which was reflected in the 1996 study of design education by Ernest Boyer and Lee Mitgang of the Carnegie Foundation for the Advancement of Teaching. Indeed, half a dozen studies over the past sixty-five years have identified the same constellation of problems that the "Boyer report" uncovered, providing further evidence of the design culture's power to resist certain kinds of change.

Such resistance, of course, is one of the roles that cultures play. Cultures are a conservative force, ballast against the rapid shifts and dramatic upheavals of the marketplace. Such conservatism may explain why practitioners, adhering to the design culture, show a relative lack of interest in matters of business. Cultures counter the movement in our society toward fragmentation and the condition that Penn State professor Christopher Clausen calls "post-culturalism." In the Summer 1996 issue of *The American Scholar*, he argues that we live in a society in which "virtually all cultural demands on individual behavior have come to seem equally outdated and meaningless." This may be why the design culture, with its influence on individual behavior—down to how we live, the cars we drive, even the pens we use—has such appeal to some. It provides a sense of identity, both individual and communal, something in which to believe.

This, in turn, may explain the difficulty of questioning the design culture in the United States, if only the most dysfunctional and self-defeating aspects of it. True believers don't question. Yet it is precisely because I believe in the values of design that I think a critique of the culture is essential, for, as Clausen observes, cultures that cannot change will die. Because any lasting cultural change must come from within, it is necessary to look at the intellectual roots of the design culture before contemplating ways in which it might be reformed.

I have so far addressed a single American design culture, but it comprises at least three major subcultures—architecture, landscape architecture, and industrial design—that have somewhat different intellectual traditions. The architecture culture stems mainly from two seemingly divergent intellectual traditions: rationalism and idealism. Architecture's studio-based pedagogy originates, in part, from eighteenth- and nineteenth-century French rationalism, which held that through the analysis of precedent and the application of reason we could arrive at a consensus about the truth in a given situation. This rationalism underlay the teaching methods of the École des Beaux-Arts, brought to the first schools of architecture in the United States by architects such as William Ware and Richard Morris Hunt. It would prove to be an odd transplant, however. As the historian David van Zanten has documented, the École served mainly to produce architects for the French bureaucracy. Government functionaries like Duban, Labrouste, and Viollet-le-Duc taught students in Paris to develop, under incredible time pressure, prototypical schemes to be detailed and built by contractors in the hinterlands, for use by faceless functionaries. Many of the features of today's design studio—the unquestioned authority of the critic, the long hours, the focus on schematic solutions, the rare discussion of users or clients—were begotten by that 150-year-old system. But only the most devoted rationalist could overlook the divergence between the École's authoritarian French context and the libertarian one in the United States.

Overlaying this rational French tradition in the architectural culture is an idealistic German one. The historian David Watkin has traced a lineage that extends from the great nineteenth-century German idealist, Georg Wilhelm Friedrich Hegel, through the work of a number of Germanic historians—Heinrich Wölfflin, Sigfried Giedion, and Rudolf Wittkower—to influential educators in America such as Walter Gropius, Mies van der Rohe, and Colin Rowe. That lineage is important because it suggests an origin for the distinctly Hegelian characteristics of the American architectural culture. The attention paid to star designers, the focus on current styles, the striving for freedom from constraints, the historicist nature of architectural theory, and the tendency to polarize education and practice all echo the Hegelian beliefs that history moves ahead through the work of a few great individuals, that every period has its characteristic styles, that history is moving toward maximizing the freedom of every person, and that cultures progress by a process of synthesizing polarities.

Landscape architecture, although it shares architecture's studio-based pedagogy, has quite different intellectual roots. They are not

French and German so much as French and English, in a tradition that ironically might be called empirical romanticism. The romanticism of the landscape culture can be traced back to Jean-Jacques Rousseau, who turned eighteenth-century French thought on its head when he argued that we are most human in the state of nature and that culture becomes more destructive the less attuned it is to the wilderness. The idea of nature and culture being opposed, and of nature as a model or at least a refuge from culture, lies at the heart of landscape architecture and at the core of the work of the first American landscape architect, Frederick Law Olmsted Sr.

The landscape culture also has its roots in the empiricism of eighteenth-century thinkers such as John Locke. Although he rarely talked about the landscape directly, Locke frequently used it as a metaphor for what he was doing: clearing the tangled underbrush, as he liked to say, of traditional ways of looking at the world and creating a new empirical landscape in which things would be seen as they really are. But there is more than metaphor involved here. Locke established a tradition, stronger in the culture of landscape design than it is in architecture, of understanding the science of soil and plants and water that underlay the aesthetics of nature. Those twin interests of the landscape culture—how nature works and what it means—are evident in the work of most landscape architects as they are in the work of most writers about nature, from Henry David Thoreau and William Burroughs to Annie Dillard and Michael Pollan.

Industrial design, the third mind-set within the design culture, stems from what might be called an Arts and Crafts empiricism. It shares with landscape architecture a connection to English empiricism, to a fascination with how things work. But, more than either architecture or landscape architecture, industrial design also draws from the English Arts and Crafts traditions, with its idea of the designer not in the studio but on the shop floor, working side by side with craftspeople or fabricators.

This is, admittedly, a greatly simplified view of the design culture's various facets. All of the subcultures share features and a part of the history of each other. And there are many examples of designers who have crossed boundaries: architects who have adopted industrial design methods, landscape architects who have embraced historicist urban design, and industrial designers who have designed environments. I have tried to sketch out the design culture in this rough form because only by understanding its intellectual roots will we be able to see the obstacles that may prevent us from working together or being more effective in the larger community.

One such obstacle has to do simply with the different assumptions we make based upon our different intellectual traditions. Rationalism, idealism, empiricism, and romanticism are commonly thought to be incompatible positions, and they do sometimes get in the way when designers try to do interdisciplinary work. Yet what is interesting about the design culture is its willingness to cross boundaries, to embrace rational idealists or empirical romantics, and to find solutions to seemingly incompatible positions. That is an advantage as the larger culture moves toward what I describe elsewhere in this collection as a "world of flows," one that is increasingly skeptical of boundaries and "turf." In a world of flows, design becomes a way of seeing patterns and connections and of integrating discrete activities into larger cycles. These could be a building cycle, as in planning, designing, constructing, and maintaining facilities, or an information cycle of discovering, synthesizing, communicating, and applying knowledge, or even an educational cycle of teaching, research, and community service as integrated and increasingly simultaneous activities. Indeed, design can play a crucial synthesizing role in a world that seeks to bridge proliferating specialties and subspecialties.

Another obstacle to our being more effective in the world has to do with our particular intellectual traditions blinding us to alternative modes of operation. For example, we commonly think of design as a visual art that progresses through a series of styles. That tradition can be traced back to Hegel. He thought architecture, whose styles represented the zeitgeist or spirit of their time, was the lowest of the arts because such things as function and construction corrupted it. Hegel also thought that architecture could be made more pure if it became more like painting and sculpture, the product of a visually oriented and visionary heroic individual. There is obviously some sense to this. Design does involve visual perception and there are stylistic similarities among work in a given period. But the analogy of design and painting has also created problems for us. We have difficulty discussing the "art" of what we do in terms that are not visual or formal. We have difficulty integrating matters of function and construction into design without feeling that they might inhibit our creativity, and we have difficulties working in teams or communicating what we do because of our self-perception as visionary individuals.

At the time Hegel was working, Goethe suggested another way of looking at design. He wrote to a friend in 1829, "I have found among my papers a sheet ... in which I call architecture frozen music." Goethe's analogy has typically been interpreted from a visual point of view, looking at the rhythm or modulation or harmony of elements in buildings. I am interested in something else that it suggests, which has received little attention: to consider design as a performing art, rather than a visual one.

There are aspects of the performing arts that have long been of interest to design. We obviously act as stage setters, creating spaces or environments in which people interact. Indeed, in recent decades, some designers have taken that metaphor quite literally: Lawrence Halprin's idea of the landscape architect as choreographer or Charles Moore's treatment of buildings as stage sets. At the same time, the idea of the signature designer—akin to a rock star or a movie idol—has taken hold. We have been, in other words, looking at performance mainly in terms that already fit our culture: set design is the one analogy that most closely aligns with our self-conception as a visual art, while the performance star most closely fits our emphasis on individual vision.

These are not necessarily inappropriate analogies, but what may hold the greatest value for the design culture is rather its deep affinity to the performing arts, which has remained largely unexplored and, more important, which offers some ways out of the cultural predicaments we encounter. For instance, unlike the notion of an individual creation prevalent in most of the visual arts, the performing arts offer a model of an inherently interdisciplinary, collaborative art form. Buildings or landscapes, as we know, never arise from the mind or hands of one person. In that sense, they are not like a painting or a sculpture, but rather more like putting on a play, involving designers, contractors, consultants, and clients much as staging a drama involves writers, performers, lighting/set/costume designers, and a receptive audience. We sometimes act as if interaction with contractors, consultants, and clients works against the "art" of what we do, and if we think of ourselves only as visual artists that might be true. But the performing arts give us a model and a body of theory that show that the multidisciplinary aspect of design need not deny "art." In fact, collaboration *is* the art of design.

At the same time, thinking about design as a type of performance probably comes closer to how the public (as opposed to the profession) actually perceives what we do. The analogy to painting or sculpture has encouraged us to view design projects as objects or sites to be contemplated in isolation, a mentality evident in the way we often photograph projects devoid of people, removed from their physical context, and frozen in time, usually just after completion. But, as J. B. Jackson has argued in *A Sense of Place, A Sense of Time*, most people see the designed environment over time, and value it according to how it performs and what meaningful events have occurred in it. A score or script cannot consistently generate bad performances and be considered good, nor can composers or playwrights remain relevant if they ignore how people use, interpret, or respond to their work over time. Thinking about the performance of what we create as designers is not someone else's problem; it is one of the most important design problems, one that others less qualified are willing to attend to if we continue to walk away from it.

Finally, a visual art assumes that the viewer understands the meaning of what is depicted, a perennial frustration for the design community since the public has so little education in the codified meaning of designed forms and symbols. The public's low design literacy arises from a number of causes that lie beyond our control, such as the lack of attention given to design in most elementary and secondary schools. There is no doubt, however, that the lack of public awareness also stems from the design culture's neglect of oral and written communication, which underlie most public discourse.

While we should continue to try to educate the public about the formal aspects of what we do, we cannot assume that visual communication is enough. Here, too, we might gain from thinking of ourselves as a performing art, in which the ability to communicate to an audience is paramount. Inculcating the idea of design as a performing as well as a visual art suggests that as educators we should attend to how students communicate to various audiences, how they work together on projects as a cast, and how they address the performance of what they do as well as its form.

Our pedagogy itself is inextricable from any critique of the design culture. While clients and communities, unwilling to coddle designers, have prompted some self-examination and expansion of services among design firms, the greatest resistance to change remains in the schools, which have, for too long, tried to preserve the design culture and pass it on to the next generation.

The idea of a world of flows suggests that in academia, too, we begin to use our synthesizing and pattern-finding skills to make connections with related and even seemingly unrelated disciplines in the university, as well as with disparate and even sometimes discordant groups in the community. That envisions design as a way of structuring fluid relationships, as fundamental a way of thinking as science or logic. Rather than the conservative force they represent now, the schools should instead be the place where the critique of the design culture is most acute. That, I believe, is their cultural role.

One of the most memorable lectures of my college years was given by Colin Rowe in an architectural theory class, when he talked about the hedgehogs and foxes of architecture. Rowe admitted to borrowing the idea from the late Oxford historian of ideas, Isaiah Berlin. In an essay published in 1951 entitled "The Hedgehog and the Fox," Berlin had used the distinction made by the Greek poet Archilochus—"The fox knows many things, but the hedgehog knows one big thing"—as a way of understanding a fundamental difference in the ways people think. Berlin argued that thinkers such as Plato, Dante, Hegel, and Nietzsche were "hedgehogs" who see the world in terms of one big idea, be it Form, Faith, Freedom, or Power respectively in the case of those just mentioned. Aristotle, Shakespeare, Montaigne, Goethe, and Joyce were "foxes," according to Berlin. They saw the world as endlessly diverse, full of conflicting ideas and values that will never fit into a single whole.

Berlin seemed most interested in those who, like Leo Tolstoy, pretended to be one type of thinker while really being the other. "Tolstoy," observed Berlin, "was by nature a fox, but believed in being a hedgehog," writing about the complexities of human relationships in books like *War and Peace*, yet producing highly simplistic polemics like his book *What Is Art?* Such thinkers may have interested Berlin because he could have described himself that way. Berlin was one of the great foxlike thinkers of our time, with an encyclopedic knowledge of Western thought and a keen understanding of the irreconcilable conflicts in human values. But in finding such conflicts virtually everywhere he looked, Berlin sounded, at times, very much the hedgehog.

Something of the same could be said of Colin Rowe. He, too, has been one of the great foxes of architecture, valuing the formal diversity of architecture and articulating an urban theory premised on it in books like *Collage City*. And yet, if architecture is deemed nothing but diverse, and the city is always considered a collage, that in itself constitutes one overarching idea. In other words, if a fox only sees other foxes, is it acting like a hedgehog?

In *Collage City*, Rowe and his coauthor, Fred Koetter, observe that "Palladio is a hedgehog, Giulio Romano a fox; Hawksmoor, Soane, Philip Webb are probably hedgehogs, Wren, Nash, Norman Shaw almost certainly foxes." Among Modern architects, however, Rowe and Koetter see a definite tilt toward the hedgehog view. Frank Lloyd Wright, Walter Gropius, Mies van der Rohe, Hannes Meyer, and Buckminster Fuller each advocated one big idea, be it organicism or functionalism or technological determinism. Le Corbusier, however, comes across as the Tolstoy of architecture, acting like a fox when designing houses of great diversity, and like a hedgehog when designing cities according to one big idea. Le Corbusier, claim Rowe and Koetter, presents "another case of a fox assuming hedgehog disguises for the purposes of public appearance."

If hedgehog thinking dominated Modern architecture, you could say that foxes have definitely invaded the architectural henhouse over the past three decades or so. The very fact that we now commonly talk about the increasing complexity of the world we work in and the growing diversity of the people we work for demonstrates the foxlike character of late modern and postmodern architecture. To hold forth with the one big idea now seems naïve or, worse, repressive. But hedgehog thinkers still exist among us, and foxes and hedgehogs still disguise themselves as one another for the sake of public appearance.

Consider Paul Rudolph and Aldo Rossi. Formally, the work of those two architects stood poles apart. Rudolph's interest in intricate spaces, asymmetrical forms, and textured surfaces differed decidedly from Rossi's tendency to use simple spaces, symmetrical forms, and unadorned surfaces. Both were hedgehogs, however, in the way that they stuck to their positions in the face of changing tastes, varied programs, and occasionally withering criticism. Both held on to their own big ideas to the very end.

Nevertheless, neither was above putting on the disguise of the fox for public purposes. In Rudolph's case, that disguise was manifested in the sheer complexity of his buildings, whose interpenetrating spaces appeared to accommodate diverse needs and varied demands. In reality, many of Rudolph's buildings handle diverse programs rather poorly, with many different functions crammed into spaces that open on to each other, often with nothing but a change in level separating them. Rossi's disguise took the form of words. In his book *The Architecture of the City*, Rossi sounds like a fox in his praise of the "structural complexity" of cities, but he went on, in the book and in his own buildings, to search for the universal types, the streets, squares, colonnades, and so on, that underpin that complexity—thus revealing his true hedgehog self.

A couple of ironies emerge from the example of Rudolph and Rossi. While foxlike thinking supposedly tolerates diverse opinions and positions, the need of closet hedgehogs to disguise themselves as foxes suggests that some of the foxes among us may be less tolerant than we think. Obversely, foxlike thinking, taken too far, can blind us to connections that might be less apparent. Not only did Rudolph and Rossi share a similar hedgehog resistance to changing taste, but also their work, despite its formal differences, grew out of a similar reaction to Modernism. If all we see are differences, we close ourselves off from ever seeing commonalities.

Foxes may now dominate architectural thought, but that has not inhibited some from acting like hedgehogs. Consider architects such as Robert Venturi and Peter Eisenman. As with Rudolph and Rossi, the work of Venturi and Eisenman looks nothing alike. The interest of Venturi and his partner, Denise Scott Brown, in representational pop art has led them to a flattened, narrative-driven, cartoonlike architecture, while Eisenman's interest in abstract poststructuralist aesthetics has generated buildings with a fragmented, three-dimensional, weblike character. Despite stylistic differences, these architects share a suspicion of utopia and an attraction to complexity. The seeing of many things has become, for them, the one big idea.

But that hedgehog mentality may be just a disguise. Robert Venturi opens his book *Complexity and Contradiction* by positing his foxlike interests in personal terms: "I like complexity and contradiction in architecture." Five paragraphs later, he holds up that personal credo as a total solution: "But an architecture of complexity and contradiction has a special obligation toward the whole: its truth must be in its totality or implications of totality." A hedgehog for public appearance? Peter Eisenman has employed a similar strategy in a more foxlike way. He has pursued, in much of his architecture, notions of absence and randomness, and he has criticized the age-old connection of form to content or function as the "trap of immanence, of using a moral argument ... to justify the making of form." He then slyly holds up his point of view as itself the only immanent one: "a concept of the formal would have no immanent or original relationship to its content, and it is the absence of these relationships that would become its only immanence."

The architectural foxes among us have received more attention in recent years than the hedgehogs, a reflection perhaps of the growing diversity of people in our culture. Yet, it is significant that many architects still feel the urge to adopt, like Tolstoy or Le Corbusier, the disguise of the hedgehog, to put on the cloak of the visionary whose one big idea everyone will follow. That urge may be just the fading echo of Modernism, with its multiple choice of utopias, each presented by its proponent as having the answer to all of our problems. Or it may be the result of truly respecting diversity: if we are to act like the fox, we must recognize that even the hedgehog has a point. And that while the former may appeal to our sense of fairness and equity, the latter offers what it takes—paraphrasing one of the great hedgehogs of architecture, Daniel Burnham—to stir our souls.

Which brings me back to the original fragment from Archilochus's poem, later developed into a Greek fable that goes something like this: the wily fox brags to the single-minded hedgehog about having many ways of outsmarting hounds, but when hunting dogs approach the two, the hedgehog simply hides in his hole, while the fox, uncertain which of his many tricks to use, gets caught. It is possible, concludes the fable, to be too clever for your own good, a word of caution that all of us (including those who seek meaning in fables) should take to heart.

Another fable, this one by Aesop, offers a caution also relevant to the architect working in this postmodern era. Called "The Stag at a Pool," the fable tells of a male deer standing at the water's edge admiring his large antlers and bemoaning his skinny legs and small hooves, when he hears some hunters and their dogs approaching. The stag's legs, which he had just faulted, serve him well in running away from danger, but the antlers, of which he was so proud, become entangled in a thicket, allowing the dogs and hunters to overtake him. Aesop ends with the injunction that we should look to use before ornament.

Note that Aesop does not argue for use without ornament, as a functionalist might. Instead, he asks us to consider the order of our priorities, to find the proper balance between use and ornament, and to know when we need more of one or the other. Has our tendency to reduce the complexity of architecture to a singular issue, be it modern functionalism or postmodern ornamentalism, contributed to our discipline being overtaken by the dogs and hunters at our heels? The latter, of course, being developers and contractors who want to relegate design to a minor role in the building process, or engineers and interior designers who want to practice architecture of a sort, without even knowing what they don't know.

The fable also forces us to ask how much the pool, or the architectural media in our case, has affected our view of ourselves. Like a pool, the media invariably distorts an image because of the interpretation it always entails and because of the limits of its own medium, which allows it to depict that which lends itself to visual or verbal description, and to avoid that which doesn't, such as the feel of a place. The stag's ornament—his antlers—contributed to his being caught, but so did the amount of time he spent admiring himself in the pool rather than being ready to move. Less regard for the mirror and more regard for our ability to change seem implicit in Aesop's fable and certainly relevant to architects' situation today.

Despite the apparent changes going on in architecture, with new forms and products emerging every month, our discipline is relatively resistant to real change, to transformations in what we do or in how we relate to others. The antlers that catch us in the thicket may be less the literal ornament on our buildings, and more the figural ornament of the professional license, which frees us to do some things but also constrains us from doing others. By equating the architect with the design of buildings, we close off the tremendous opportunities that exist in the design of nonbuildings, as in public policy, human organizations, virtual environments, and the like. What will put us out of the reach of those who pursue us is our mode of thinking, rather than a particular application of it in the form of building design. The latter may hold more visual appeal when we gaze at it, as in a pool, but the former is by far the more useful, the real legs of our discipline.

Another Aesop fable of relevance is called "The Great and Little Fishes." It is about a group of fishermen who, drawing in their nets, catch all of the big fish, while letting the small fish swim away. Aesop concludes from this that our insignificance is often the cause of our safety, but I think that there is more than safety involved here. For example, if we think in terms of architectural firms rather than fish, we may discern a lesson in adaptability. Some of the best new ideas and most inspired new work in architecture occur when architects are relatively unknown—small fish not yet caught in the net of conventional thinking.

Unfortunately, good architects have difficulty remaining small fry. Even if their firms don't get numerically larger, they loom larger in the public eye, gaining media attention and plum commissions. They then face the same threat confronting every big fish, of becoming trapped in the net of public and professional expectations, constrained by the signature style that they themselves created. This is why the work of so many architects declines in quality and vitality once they become famous, and only those willing to give up on what they once represented and start over—Le Corbusier and Wright come immediately to mind—seem able to avoid the fate of big fish.

Big firms, like big-name architects, have a similar dilemma. They can become quickly caught in what they have always done and get swallowed up in the competition. However, large firms can avoid that fate if they think and act like a collection of small firms, each able to respond quickly to changing conditions or new opportunities and each willing to cultivate new talent and let it rise to the top. The greatest hurdle large firms have to overcome is a conceptual one, first propounded by Daniel Burnham in the mid-1890s. Burnham recommended that large firms should organize themselves like the large corporations they served. The resulting structure, with owners at the top of a hierarchy making most of the decisions, defined large organizations for decades, but it no longer works well for corporations in a fast-moving global economy, and it no longer works well for architectural firms, either.

If there is a moral here, it is that there are few certainties. Small fish can get big and slow, while big fish can act small and nimble and thus survive. Perhaps the only thing for certain is that you want to do everything you can to avoid nets altogether. One of the public obligations of a profession is to seek to improve people's lives and to develop new knowledge with that in mind, and that can't happen if we are trapped in someone else's net or in one of our own making.

That brings me to the last fable, "The Leopard and the Fox," also by Aesop. In it, the two animals have a contest to determine which is the finer creature. The leopard emphasizes the beauty of its coat, with its many spots, but the fox ends up winning the competition by pointing out that it is better to have a versatile mind than a variegated body. Architecture these days is full of variegated bodies, buildings with attractive wrappings but little meaning. Our profession has begun to lose the competition with other fields not because our fees are too high or our buildings too expensive, but because we have not been versatile enough in our thinking about the true needs of our clients and of the public and about innovative ways to address those needs.

In the Scheme of Things

There are those in the profession who argue that architects have no choice but to focus on the appearance of buildings. They point out that building owners, zoning officials, and even neighborhood groups increasingly make many of the crucial decisions about what a building is to be, how big it should be, and approximately where it should stand. Any architect who ignores such constraints, they say, is not going to survive very long.

To a certain extent that argument is true. But what it overlooks is the role of the architect in questioning the givens of a project or the assumed needs of an owner. That role emerges from our education, which unlike that of many other professions teaches us to think broadly rather than narrowly, to cross disciplinary boundaries rather than to enforce them, to find optimum solutions rather than correct answers. Such a thought process is so integral to architectural education that we often forget its uniqueness and its applicability not just to the design of buildings, but also to all of the assumptions and constraints that impinge upon the design process. We learn in school to constantly question our design decisions, so why accept, passively, the decisions of clients or officials?

The great Modern architects knew this. We tend to focus on the forms of their work, almost as if they have a mystical power we might absorb if we study them hard enough. The power of their work, however, arose not from some mysterious ability to make forms, but from their constant questioning of the world as they found it and their determination to act on the answers.

Too much architecture today is too leopardlike, too superficially attractive or visually compelling, without the content that comes from grappling with the real problems of our time. And too much of architectural education focuses on the discipline's internal arguments rather than on contemporary concerns and how the physical environment relates to them. It matters not whether one addresses a range of issues or focuses on just one; some of the greatest architects of this century, as we've seen, had a single vision that informed everything they did and sustained them throughout their careers. So let us honor not the leopards, but the hedgehogs and the foxes in our midst, not the variegated bodies, but the versatile minds that, despite all the distractions, manage to hold on to their own guiding fables.

The **Redesign** of Practice

As a magazine editor, I spent years visiting architectural firms, and while most architects eagerly showed me their work, very few ever talked about their practices. When I inquired about the latter, I would hear virtually the same thing: whether busy or not, practitioners admitted that profits or compensation could be better. Why, I wondered, did the architectural profession accept this situation as if nothing could be done about it? Why did well-educated, highly experienced, extremely knowledgeable professionals tolerate incomes lower than those in fields requiring less schooling and much less risk? Why did we seem so fatalistic about our practices when we often show such confidence in finding design solutions to almost any problem our clients present us with?

One reason, I think, has to do with the compartmentalized way we view design and practice. Most schools encourage us to think of design and practice as separate realms, relegating the practice "support" courses to the end of the curriculum, long after students have come to think of design as the making of form and the shaping of space. Likewise, the specialization so characteristic of higher education discourages those who teach the practice courses from connecting their subject to what students learn in design studio.

The division between design and practice carries into the work world. Few partners think of applying to the organization and operation of the firm the same creativity employed in their architectural work. As a result, the design of the firm often has no connection to the design work produced by the office: avant-garde architects frequently run the most conservatively structured work environments. We cannot blame individual offices and schools for this disconnect between design and practice. They are part of a culture in architecture that has maintained this split for a long time, and part of a mind-set that can be traced back centuries to divisions, in Western culture at least, between art and business, thinking and doing, gentry and merchants. Questioning these false dichotomies is what every architectural firm and school must do if it is to thrive in the coming years.

Architectural practice, in short, has become one of the major design problems of our time. While addressing this problem will demand changes in how we practice, it must begin with a redefinition of design. By defining design in the narrowest and most conventional terms, such as giving form to environments or objects, we have created an unnecessary obstacle for ourselves, limiting the application of our knowledge and, not coincidentally, limiting the influence of our discipline. If, instead, we see design as the finding of optimal solutions to difficult and complex problems, then the notion of designing architectural practice becomes comprehensible, part of a continuum of design thinking that need not stop with our own offices or even our own discipline. The question then becomes, How do we apply design thinking to practice?

As with any design problem, we must begin by defining its nature. What needs must we address? What context must we work within? What means do we have at our disposal? The conditions in which most firms now practice have given a sense of urgency to such questions. The context surrounding the architectural profession has changed so much in recent years that many offices now find it difficult to achieve even the most basic motivations for professional practice: personal satisfaction, professional respect, and profit. Until we first understand these contextual changes, we cannot define our needs or how we might accommodate them.

One of the major changes surrounding practice involves the decreasing input and influence that architects now have in projects. Earlier in this century, as soon as clients had perceived the need for a building, they typically commissioned an architect to help them through the process. Now, other entities, including accountants, contractors, and developers, have become dominant at the front end of the building process, guiding clients through decisions about such things as location, siting, size, function, and financing, all of which have a tremendous impact on the final outcome of a project. Architects, in turn, have been pushed back in the schedule, having less influence over critical early decisions. Not only has this shift in power produced a lot of bad buildings, but it has resulted in architects adding less value and so commanding lower fees and less respect.

Another critical change in the context of architectural practice has been a reduction in the control we have over our work. Related to the timing of our involvement in projects, this change stems from a shift in many clients' perception of us. Certainly one way in which program managers, construction managers, and project managers make themselves look good in the eyes of a client and help justify their fees is to disparage the architect who traditionally provided such services. As a result, more and more clients have over time come to see architects as unable to control projects and in need of outside management. Our profession is not alone in this. The management of professionals has become a booming business, as doctors know when they have to get permission from HMOs to recommend procedures or as lawyers know when corporate accountants require them to bid for work or to cap the number of hours spent on a case. In construction, this has created a situation in which the architect, once the leader of the building team, has been relegated to the role of just another participant, often with remarkably little control over decisions about the work. We have sometimes been our own worst enemy: the gradual reduction of our responsibilities in the standard contracts we ourselves issue has aided our marginalization. But we are not the only losers; the public loses as well, as the focus on the bottom lines of budget and schedule degrades the quality of the environment we all live in.

A third change in the context of architectural practice has to do with the time allowed to do our work. The less influence and control we have, the more likely others, who may not be aware of what architects actually do, will determine how much time we have to work. The increasing pace of our work reflects a similar expectation across the entire economy, fueled by information technology and automated systems of various sorts that operate at a speed (and a stupidity) unmatched by humans. The computer, like most technology, has made practice easier at one level and much more difficult at another, and we, as a profession and as citizens, have not addressed the difficulties nearly enough. Along with clients' expectations for ever-faster service, there exists an expectation of error-free performance on the part of professionals. This reflects the quest, also pervasive in modern culture, for certainty, perfectibility, and infallibility. At a time when clients can insure themselves against almost anything, they increasingly want the same insurance in the very complicated and risky business of construction, often at the expense of architects and their insurers. Any delay, any error, and we pay.

The changing context of architecture in many ways defines the needs that any redesign of practice must address. We need to find ways to advance our design input to earlier stages of the decision-making process, we need to improve our control of project budgets and schedules, and we need to defend the time that the design process requires to produce the desired results. At the same time, we must use as leverage what means we have to address these problems, since clients or other disciplines are unlikely to do it for us. Here, the division between design and practice has become most acute. While we doggedly pursue ways of achieving aesthetic goals in buildings, we act rather timidly in the pursuit of public policy changes that would enable us to reach no less ambitious goals in practice. The main channel for such changes, the American Institute of Architects, generally sees its responsibility rather narrowly, pursuing legislation that will benefit architects in the short term, such as increasing investment in buildings or cities, defending architects' professional turf, and so on. Proposing any effective public policy that addresses the broader changes in the context of practice has yet to happen.

A small but growing number of architectural firms have not waited for the professional association to act. They have, instead, begun to redefine what they do and to redesign the way they do it. While this has occurred across a broad spectrum of practice, this redesign falls into roughly four groups.

Firms that have redefined the geography of practice constitute the first group. Operating at an international scale, such firms, as they have come in contact with other cultures and other modes of practice, have had to reenvision who they are, what they have to offer, and how they operate. The notion of a firm doing work overseas is not new; throughout the twentieth century, the largest offices have operated across the globe, sometimes with branch offices in foreign lands and other times by using the telephone and mail to communicate with associate architects on location. In previous decades, that geographical spread had relatively little impact on the design of the firm itself.

Now, we see hybrid organizations of various kinds emerging, all with globalism in mind. Some firms have used electronic technology to treat distant offices as contiguous with their own, employing computer modems to dispatch drawings back and forth so that projects can be worked on around the clock. This addresses the desire of clients for the super-fast production of documents and the need of firms to be more productive and thus better paid. A similar approach, equally dependent upon electronics and telecommuting, is the "virtual" firm.

Such firms exist across a wide territory without there being a central office or, in some cases, a central firm at all. Smaller firms especially have begun to form strategic alliances or affiliations that allow each to still practice independently in their local area, but to compete together on larger projects, to share information among themselves, and to complement the expertise of each other. They can thus achieve the economy of scale enjoyed by large firms but without the overhead, sometimes maintaining only a small front office with meeting rooms and a reception area in which to greet clients.

While similar in their use of technology, these two approaches differ in an important way. The global firms, like those in the communications and financial industries, have discovered that their value increases with their ability to move information or data rapidly and to keep it flowing twenty-four hours a day. Because we associate architecture with the making of large, physical objects, we tend not to think of our field as primarily an information activity, but that is what it has largely become, and the global firms have recognized that fact. The "virtual" firms have used as leverage a different advantage: the need in the global economy to respond rapidly to changing demands. These firms bring together teams of experts to address a particular problem or to apply a highly developed skill, disbanding the group once the needs of a particular client are met. They have, in essence, expanded what most architectural firms do already in assembling consultants to work on buildings.

A second group includes firms that have redesigned themselves by expanding the services they offer. This comes, in part, because of the incursions that others outside the field—construction managers, engineers, interior designers—have made upon the traditional turf of architects. At the front end of the design process, program managers, competition consultants, strategic planners, and a host of others have positioned themselves to divert clients before they ever reach the architect, offering guidance at the inception of projects with little of the regulation, less of the liability, and none of the licensure requirements that architects face. A smattering of architectural firms have responded to this competition by offering clients strategic planning, facility analysis, even real estate and development advice. Such services have attracted higher fees than those typically paid to architects, and for some firms this work has grown faster than any other part of their practice. Larger firms have added staff to provide these services; smaller offices have done so by developing networks that include disciplines such as finance and organizational management. This diversity of disciplines creates a challenge in offices, in getting professionals with different values, expectations, and languages to communicate and collaborate effectively. But success in offering front-end services requires such communication, since firms cannot reasonably offer strategic services if they, themselves, cannot act in coordination.

Meanwhile, facility managers and building operations specialists of various kinds have begun to populate the once-undeveloped areas beyond the building's delivery, providing services over the life of the building rather than, as architects have traditionally done, up to the point of the structure's completion. The property at the back end of the design process covers much more territory than what architects have traditionally occupied. Buildings last a long time and their upkeep and operation demand ongoing services, which differ from the relatively short burst of activity that constitutes design and construction. Facilities managers have not competed with architects so much as taken a lot of turf that the profession might have staked out for itself.

Some architects have taken the initiative in this regard. Offering facilities management services, these firms have learned that staying involved with clients, in the way lawyers counsel clients for years, has long-term benefits, generating an extraordinary amount of repeat work. In one firm, over 80 percent of its work is repeat business because of the office's ongoing relationship with clients as their facilities manager. Much of this repeat work, as well as much facilities management, lacks glamour, but such services position firms to get the major commissions when they do appear because of the office's proven track record and knowledge of the client company.

The blurring of the architectural profession's traditional boundaries brings us to a third approach that many firms have taken in the redesign of practice: expanding the discipline itself. Despite the often broad interests of architects, the profession tends to look inward, rarely engaging in discussion with other fields. A number of firms, though, have begun to embrace other disciplines seemingly far removed from what architects do. Some firms, for example, now employ computer scientists to develop software, graphic designers to offer corporate identity services, and experts in areas such as health care or education to solidify their position in the design of particular building types. More unconventional partnerships have arisen as well. One firm, focusing on the design of "healthy" buildings, includes a physician who examines the components of proprietary materials to gauge their effects on users' health. Another, providing security services, includes a criminologist and a specialist on terrorism.

Such partnerships reveal a dilemma at the heart of the architectural profession: the question of specialization. Some argue that we must all become more specialized in order to thrive, while others feel that our strength rests with our being one of the last generalist professions. To a certain degree, both sides are right. Our interdisciplinary problem-solving skills do set us apart from other professions, although most clients also value us according to the extent of our specialized knowledge, seeking out firms that have done other projects just like the one under consideration. The resolution seems to lie in bringing a generalist's insight to specialized knowledge, enhancing the latter without losing the former.

A fourth area in which architects have begun to redesign practice involves not expanding, but regrading the profession's own turf. Our turf has traditionally had three distinct regions occupied by different kinds of firms—design firms focused on form and aesthetics, service firms geared to responding to clients' needs, and production firms structured to turn out contract documents quickly and efficiently. Clients, however, have come to expect all three: fast delivery, attentive service, and good design. That, in turn, has led a number of firms to reexamine their practices to eliminate inefficiencies and speed up the process, while still producing high-quality work.

At one large firm, the designers have institutionalized a preschematic phase in which they generate a strong, simple concept for the project that all team members understand and support, which speeds up later design stages and which informs the decisions everyone makes through the completion of the project. (This firm wins design awards from the profession and service awards from client groups.) At the other extreme in terms of design, but not profit, is an equally large firm that has developed a "kit of parts" for the particular kind of building they specialize in, enabling them to generate a site plan within twenty-four hours of the client's first visit and design drawings in a week or so. Both of these firms indicate that the once-clear lines between different types of offices have begun to blur. Design firms can be very service oriented, service firms very production oriented.

Such firms raise a question about the relationship of architectural practice and time. Most architectural schools inculcate a culture in which time seems infinitely expandable, or rather, expendable, with "all-nighters" viewed as a badge of honor, a necessary induction into the club. This quaint view runs up against a world in which all work has had to become more productive, to accomplish more in less time. Some argue that design cannot be tethered to the clock, that creative ideas do not always come when summoned. But other creative fields—writing and journalism, for example—defy that myth, as their practitioners have learned to create under tight deadlines. Architects must learn to do the same. The schools need to put more emphasis on time management and architectural offices need to find ways to increase the pace of design and production, without affecting quality.

How successful have these various redesign efforts been? A few firms report higher profits, faster growth, and better compensation. The profession, however, has yet to engage in a rigorous "postoccupancy" evaluation of the changes occurring in practice. The absence of such analysis is a reflection, perhaps, of our general inability to evaluate buildings after the fact for fear of exposing mistakes and for lack of funds for such work. If we are to improve our lot as a profession, we must find a way to describe and evaluate the diversity of our methods. The same is true if we are to improve our lot as designers. In analyzing the design of our practices, we will begin to discover how design thinking relates to all forms of human action and organization, not just in our own offices but in those of our clients. All too often, clients need not just a new building but a new identity for their products or services, new ways of organizing and motivating employees, a new way of making or delivering product. All of these needs also involve design, and when we see all such operations as within the architect's purview, we will have reached a significant turning point in the profession. We will no longer be just building form-givers, but architects in the broadest sense of the word, which, I would argue, is our rightful place in the world.

Babel Revisited

A colleague of mine once said that whenever her contractor father used the word architect, it was always prefaced with the expletive "goddamned." Most of us shrug off such terms of endearment, so often do we hear them. But the way in which members of the building industry talk about each other contributes to its being one of the most fragmented and adversarial industries, comprising many small operations that look upon each other with suspicion and seem all too willing to litigate.

We can no longer afford this suspicion or name-calling. Increasing numbers of clients and the public rightfully view such "intramural" conflict as a waste of time and money. As one client said to me once, lamenting the number of construction lawsuits he had endured, "The only winners are the lawyers." One of the most dangerous and stressful activities, construction requires a tremendous amount of coordination and communication. At the same time, its complexity demands a variety of operations—designing, calculating, building—aided by the specialized skills of architects, engineers, or contractors. Today's increasing pace of production and the diversifying of building-delivery methods demand further cooperation, all of which make it imperative that we learn to get along.

Certainly, the growing use of computers should encourage the sharing of information. Yet, misunderstandings remain, in no small part because of the very different cultures that we've cultivated within our industry, and which we perpetuate through the language, or rather languages, we use. We rarely think of these languages as a problem, perhaps because words interest us less than the things we build, but how we talk about ourselves and what we do as a result affects the way we think and view our world. Listen to the conversations at a construction site some day and you'll wonder how anything ever gets built, as the contractor talks about how to construct something, the architect about how it should look, the engineer about how big it should be, and the client about what it will cost. It's as if we had taken to heart what the philosopher Ludwig Wittgenstein once wrote: "The limits of my language are the limits of my reality."

We all know of the biblical story that traces the diversity of language and culture to the arrogance and aftermath of an architectural act: God's destruction of the Tower of Babel. In a story that Franz Kafka wrote in 1920 entitled "The City Arms," the Tower of Babel emerges not just as an affront to God, but as a prosaic parable about the nature of the construction industry. Builders from all the nations of the world assemble, in Kafka's tale, and proceed to argue about who does or gets what, "added to which was the fact that already the second or third generation recognized the meaninglessness, the futility of building a Tower unto Heaven—but all had become too involved with each other to quit." Such conflicts continue to this day. The building industry itself tends to overlook the issue. All too often we think that improved technology or techniques will make us more effective, responsive, and profitable. But we also need a better grasp of how particular jargons affect our ability to communicate. We can't work together if we misunderstand each other, and yet that is precisely what we have done, since Babel.

My first exposure to the dialect of design came during architecture school, where my professors, none of them French, used a set of French words—*parti*, *charrette*, *enfilade*—to describe physical and procedural elements of the design process. As entering freshmen, we still used simple, strong, Anglo-Saxon words—door, window, wall—to describe our work. Just months after entering school, we had also been initiated into the architectural club, whose membership demanded that we use the language of our professors. Doors became entry nodes; windows, fenestration. One professor told us to think like architects, which I now realize meant we should talk like them, in a lingo only other architects could understand.

Here, then, began our separation as architects from the contractors, engineers, and consultants we would have to work with when we graduated, and for whom our high-flown French words would sound as fatuous as they are foreign. Those words, in school, served to build an identity and sense of community among us, which had their value. As the linguist George Steiner put it, "a language builds a wall around the 'middle kingdom' of the group's identity. It is secret towards the outsider and inventive of its own world." But we did not learn well enough how to do what Steiner considers basic to all language: we could translate our words into lines on paper and eventually into built structures, but translating them into other more common words never seemed important enough. Given the obscurity of so much of the current architectural discourse it would appear that for many of us clear communication is still not important enough.

After architecture school, I took a year off to design and build an addition to my parents' house, largely by myself. While the project made me realize the limits of my manual skills, I admired the tools of construction and the words that described them—plane, level, plumb—each of which worked as both a noun and a verb, as both the thing itself and the action it involved. It was around that time that I came across Wittgenstein's analogy of language and tools. "Think of the tools in a toolbox," he wrote. "There is a hammer, pliers, a saw, a screwdriver, a rule, a gluepot, glue, nails, and screws. The functions of words are as diverse as the functions of these objects."

I occupied my mind, as the building of the addition did my hands, thinking of words that coincided with such tools. I imagined hammer words that try to smash the opposition, such as "bore" in the phrase "less is a bore"; pliers words that try to pinch together ideas that don't necessarily go together, like "critical regionalism" or "deconstructivism"; screwdriver words that try to fasten down notions that elude any such effort, like "*genius loci*" or "postfunctionalism"; or glue words that seem to stick to everything, like "tectonic" or "contextual." We have used such word-tools to build the structure we call "architecture," and yet I wonder how well we have understood them or their effect on us.

After the completion of the addition, I began working in a historic preservation office, where I identified, researched, and described historic buildings. I found myself thrown into yet another language, that of architectural history, with its arcane vocabulary, mostly French or Latin in origin: quoins, rustication, architrave, imbrication. I had many colleagues who relished such obscure words, claiming that their precision justified their use, a notion with which I largely agreed. But, in describing buildings for listing on the National Register, I soon learned that the more technical the language, the better the chance a building would be approved.

This struck me as terribly ironic. Preservation had appealed to me because I saw the past as liberating us from the binds of the present, confronting us with places and people very different from our own. Yet the preservation bureaucracy seemed to lack any sense of the freedom of our enterprise or the excitement of our discoveries. Some people I worked with measured success in the number of forms completed and the number of buildings listed, as if we traded in commodities. These bureaucrats, who worked in Washington and Philadelphia, far from the buildings they passed judgment on, practiced what the philosopher William Barrett called "the illusion of technique," in which technical knowledge and technical decisions of the most hair-splitting kind became dominant, with almost no discussion of the ideas in or meaning of the structures we sought to save. The language we had to use to describe even the most amazing structures had as much personality as the bureaucracy itself did. The book may not kill the building, despite what Victor Hugo once wrote, but bureaucratic language does. And so I fled the preservation field of those days, vowing never to kill architecture with words again.

In subsequent years I worked in a couple of architectural offices, where I encountered the babel of languages at its most intense. Among the staff in the office, the designers upheld the jargon of our school days and the production staff the vocabulary of the job site, while the partners and project managers often spoke in another idiom: that of the law. The legal language took two very different but related forms. The language in our contracts rarely referred to anything specific, as if written by people attempting to say something precise about a vague subject. "The contract," in a typical phrase in such documents, "represents the entire and integrated agreement between the parties hereto and supersedes prior negotiations, representation, or agreements, either written or oral." Such verbiage, despite its claims to precision, remains very much open to interpretation. What constitutes a "negotiation" or a "representation"? Because they don't refer to anything specific, such phrases leave plenty of room for others to claim otherwise, which, of course, creates work for more lawyers to make or refute their cases.

The vagueness of legal language has led most architects to the opposite extreme in the specifications they write. These project books consist of short, declarative statements and long, descriptive lists of things. "Water," as a standard phrase goes, "should be potable—clean and free from acids, alkalis, or deleterious amounts of organic materials." As problems are resolved in projects and as lawsuits get settled, new words are added to the overabundance of specifications, turning the latter into tomes so weighty that I wonder if contractors even read them.

This has also led to a demeaning of construction. As recently as the early twentieth century, contracts for even large projects comprised a page or two, and specifications a couple dozen pages or so, with terms such as "best practice" or "accepted standard of care" used throughout. Those documents, in other words, existed within a social setting in which architects, engineers, and contractors saw each other as colleagues able to agree upon what each expected of the other. Whether cause or effect, the increasing use of "legalese" in both contracts and specifications reflects the breakdown of that consensus over the course of the twentieth century. As architects came to trust contractors less and contractors came to sue architects and engineers more, specifications became more prescriptive and contracts more voluminous. Meanwhile, all parties have had more constraints placed on them. Architects, for instance, now only observe construction rather than supervise it, while contractors now must follow the specifications rather than improvise better ways of doing things.

We often think that the command of a language makes us smarter, but here just the opposite has occurred. Design and construction have been "dumbed down." In an economy that rewards the added value of expertise, the constricting of information and narrowing of knowledge in the construction industry has hurt us economically as well as professionally. Reversing the legalistic trend in construction remains one of the real challenges we face, a task not easily accomplished. It will happen only with the rebuilding of trust and community among parts of the industry long set against each other, but at least there are growing financial incentives to do so.

In recent years I have worked in or at the edges of academia, first as an editor of a professional journal and then as a professor and a dean. Language has been, through all of this, at the heart of my work. I have learned, for example, that no single language defines us; in order to communicate, we often have to switch languages, like clothing, depending on the circumstance or audience. I use one language when writing to professionals, another when speaking to the public, yet another when addressing students or journalists or colleagues from other fields. Unfortunately, most disciplines, including our own, use language to build walls, as Steiner observed, rather than to communicate. If anything, those who do try to translate the ideas of the discipline to others are charged with pandering to the public or trivializing the field. The babel of professional languages, in other words, has served the interests of select few very well, to the disservice of everyone else.

Ironically, the disciplines supposedly served by jargon have begun to suffer because of it. Consider the criticism that appears in the architectural magazines or academic journals, which, I must admit, I have been complicit in producing as both an editor and a writer. Although intended mainly for those in the field, architectural criticism often ends up sending mixed messages to the public in ways that work against us. The typical article in a professional magazine, for example, combines reporting on a project—what the client wanted, what the problem entailed, how the architect responded— with the author's personal opinion about its function or aesthetics.

This format has become so pervasive that we hardly notice the underlying message: the mix of fact and feeling that presents us, on the one
hand, as a problem-solving profession, making judgments based on
need, and on the other hand, as a highly opinionated profession,
making assertions based on personal taste. This has had a tremendous
effect upon public perceptions. We may curse clients who squeeze
the time allotted for design, thinking of architecture as just the solving
of functional problems, or those who think of architects solely as the
decorators of building envelopes or public spaces. But we have sown
the seeds of these perceptions by failing to emphasize the holistic
nature of our work, in which problem solving and aesthetic judgments,
as well as a host of social, economical, and cultural considerations,
are all necessary facets of design.

Another type of criticism, often employed in the profession,
focuses on the analysis of a building's form. It presents the architect
as adept at composition, at assembling forms and spaces in pleasing
ways. By neglecting a range of other issues, such as the cultural
meaning or the performance of buildings, such formalist criticism
reduces a work of architecture, however sublime, to an act of assembly
and the architect to the role of composer. This conveys two very
different impressions about us. It encourages some patron clients and
their signature architects to see the designer's role as akin to that of
an artist assembling forms according to a personal vision, the more
idiosyncratic the better. It also spurs many other clients to view the
architect as a joiner of parts selected from product catalogs or history
books, placing us, like workers in some automated factory, under
increasing pressure to produce at an ever-greater pace. Formalist

criticism, in other words, helps fuel the commodification of architecture. Artist-architects become a kind of high-end commodity, trapped by the very signature styles that made them famous, while production firms become low-end commodities, competing mainly on price or speed of service.

A third form of architectural discourse—critical theory—has had an equally paradoxical effect. Generated mostly by and for the architectural academy, such criticism has questioned Modernism's abstractness, its neglect of context, and its cultural insensitivity, and yet it perpetrates the very same sins. It, too, is often ridiculously abstract, with rarely anything concrete for readers to hold on to as they wade through its swamp of words. It, too, largely neglects its context, making references to texts that only a few readers will know or understand. And it, too, remains insensitive to the cultural differences between, say, architecture and continental philosophy, using the language of the latter in a vain attempt to shore up the former. Few clients—and few architects, for that matter—read such criticism, and so it has had relatively little effect, despite its frequently revolutionary tone. But the critical theory of architecture breeds bad habits among some students, who, in imitating their professors, graduate unable to write a clear sentence. Likewise, this form of criticism hampers the ability of architects and academics to share ideas and information, of vital importance to both.

If we are to change the fragmented and adversarial nature of our relationships with each other and turn around the public's perception of our worth and value, we must become more vigilant of the language we use and the tacit messages we transmit. We spend much of our

time designing and constructing the physical artifacts of communities—
the homes and offices and public places that enable people to form
social bonds. We now need to spend time building community within
the industry, among colleagues and former adversaries alike. That must
begin with the bricks and mortar of language, the words we choose
and the way we use them.

There once was a troubled profession. Its members had relatively modest incomes that were slow to grow. Its schools focused on the "art" of the discipline, with relatively little time or money spent on research. And competitors from other fields made inroads into its traditional areas of practice, offering clients greater convenience and speed.

The profession I am talking about is not architecture at the end of the twentieth century, but medicine in the second half of the nineteenth century, as it has been documented by historians such as Paul Starr and essayists such as Lewis Thomas. The parallel between architecture today and medicine a century ago suggests that the professional ailments architects now face—disappointing compensation, inadequate research, and growing competition— are not unprecedented, and further, that some of the cures for architecture may be found in remedies used by other professions, like medicine.

Medicine turned itself around to become one of the most highly paid, knowledgeable, and valued professions in the twentieth century. It did so by integrating practice, education, and research through the institution of the teaching hospital, which is affiliated with the medical schools and responsible for the internships of its "residents." Physicians found a way to heal the breach between pedagogy and practice in a way that enhanced their knowledge and stature as professionals. Architects need to do the same if we are to address some of the most pressing problems facing our field. We do not have institutions like hospitals that we can modify for our purposes, as physicians began to do in the nineteenth century. Instead, we have internship programs, like the Intern Development Program (IDP), which formalizes what recent graduates learn in architectural offices. A distributed form of internship nowhere near as organized or as well funded as the apparatus of medical residency, IDP has faced increasing criticism in recent years. Architects and interns alike have chafed under the bureaucracy of IDP, while many firms have resisted taking part in the program altogether.

The economy has become so competitive and the pressure to increase productivity so intense that many firms say that they can no longer afford to take on interns, train them, and risk losing them to other firms. Evidence of the crisis of internship exists in the classified ads, most of which seek employees with a minimum of three to five years experience. Firms, in other words, want people who have already gone through their internships and who are already productive, which begs the question, Who will take interns right out of school? The current construction boom has forced firms to seek newly graduated employees, but the conflict remains between their relatively low productivity and the intensifying time pressures to which firms are subjected in the marketplace.

Some of the most famous design firms, in a tradition that Frank Lloyd Wright helped establish, take on interns without pay or even, on occasion, requiring "tuition" in exchange for the "education" the "students" will receive in the office. Even among the majority of firms that do pay their interns, many do not pay overtime. Here, again, architecture parallels medicine, which has come under growing scrutiny for its exploitation of residents working around the clock for modest wages. Unlike architectural interns, however, medical residents at least have a higher potential income to look forward to after the early years of servitude.

Architects who do not pay employees at least the minimum wage or who lack institutional approval of their "credits" violate our labor laws. Meanwhile, other firms flirt with possible IRS violations when they call their interns "consultants," expecting them to work in the office during appointed hours on assigned work under the supervision of architects, even though this procedure goes against the very definition of a consultant. The vast majority of architects, of course, do not want to break the law, but the abuses show that the bridge we have built between education and practice needs substantial rebuilding, if not wholesale replacement.

A problem of a different sort is created by firms that farm out detailing and specifications to production shops in the United States and overseas. Most architecture schools assume that their graduates will learn in an office how buildings are put together, when in fact more and more production work is executed off the firm's premises, with documents sent by modem back and forth. As a result, the experience many graduates get in offices differs little from what they got in school: working on schematics and design development.

If our current system is not working very well, what might we do to improve or change it? One obvious step would be to expand the number of work-study programs, such as those of the University of Cincinnati and Rice University. Their programs help students bridge the gap between school and practice by exposing them to offices before they graduate, enabling them to bring their practical experience to bear on their academic work. If most schools took up such a curriculum, however, would there be enough firms willing or able to take in—and pay—work-study students? Would most students want to extend the already lengthy time it takes to complete an architectural education? And would most universities go along with having one department on a work-study schedule, when all of the others are not? The work-study idea has a lot to be said for it, not least that it already exists in a few schools and has proven to work. But it is a step in the right direction rather than an ideal solution.

If work-study has an admirable modesty about it, perhaps the most radical idea was put forward by Robert Gutman of Princeton University. He argued that as architectural education has had to conform to the standards of other academic departments and has become further removed from the needs of practitioners, architectural education should leave university settings altogether and return to an apprenticeship system. American architectural education, prior to the mid-nineteenth century, had no university affiliation. Those who wanted to become architects worked with those who were, and set up their own offices in due course. It remains to be seen whether a nineteenth-century model of apprenticeship would work in today's more complicated world, where many more demands are placed upon the knowledge of architects.

Professor Gutman's proposal highlights the tension that exists within the architectural schools between those who see the field as an academic discipline and those who view it primarily as a licensed profession. I doubt either camp would view Gutman's proposal with much favor, albeit for different reasons. The removal of architectural education from the universities would drastically reduce the demand for architectural educators, since the number of students interested in studying the discipline of architecture without professional training would not come close to current enrollments. The separation of professional training from higher education would put an added burden on offices to train relatively unproductive people, something that few firms can afford. We can't go back to the old atelier system, however appealing it might seem.

But we can bring the office into the school, along the lines of the Urban Innovations Group at UCLA, with students working on community projects. Having an office in a school gives educators clearer control over the process and more of an opportunity to integrate theory and practice. However, as UIG demonstrated, such an office remains vulnerable to budget cuts and has limits to the number of students it can accommodate. Also, having an office in the school does little to build a bridge to outside practitioners, and the latter may view it as an unfair competitor.

Computer technology may offer an alternative in a variation of the virtual office. As computers rapidly break down the barriers of space and distance, they could give students access to architectural offices without their being physically present, much less employees. Schools, for example, could pay a fee to firms in exchange for access to their electronic documents and production process. A student could look, electronically, over the shoulders of practitioners, watching them develop designs, produce contract documents, and even conduct site visits, with electronic cameras recording the action.

An electronically based office in a school could also work on projects at a considerable distance, working via modem and other media to connect with clients and firms. The location of a school with such a virtual office would not matter. Nor would the expense of maintaining a virtual office be as great, assuming that the computer equipment was available, as establishing a practice center or shifting funds to a teaching office. The cumulative knowledge base that would result from the storing, copying, and sharing of information among schools in the form of electronic case studies offers another pan-professional boon. The major disadvantage of the virtual architecture office lies in the loss of face-to-face contact and first hand experience.

Valuing that face-to-face contact, some educators and practitioners have begun to discuss the idea of a teaching office: students would study history and theory in school and then, for credit, work under the supervision of both architects and educators in select offices. This would let schools, with their already overcrowded curricula, shift the practice-related courses to the teaching offices without losing control of content. Because students would be working for credit, offices would have the advantage of being allowed, under the law, not to pay them. Finally, this system would bring schools and offices—educators and practitioners—closer together, as is the case in the medical profession.

Several obstacles to implementing this idea do exist, however. Will universities be willing to give up part of their tuition to reimburse teaching offices? What about rural schools, where few local firms are able to function as teaching offices? In cities, what about other firms that must compete with teaching offices for commissions when the latter have the comparative advantage of student labor working without pay? The medical profession faced similar issues and addressed them by integrating the medical schools and teaching hospitals and by involving large numbers of physicians in resident education. If inclusive enough, teaching offices can work.

Practice centers, such as the Center for Public Architecture of the Van Alen Institute, offer a variation on this idea. It involves a consortium of schools, sometimes in conjunction with local firms, foundations, and government agencies, that provides a place where students can work, for credit, on pro bono projects, with real clients and budgets, under the supervision of both practitioners and educators. This improves upon the teaching office construct in a couple of ways. First, these practice centers would not compete with other firms, since pro bono work is not something that offices generally seek out. Second, they would offer the opportunity for universities, through their schools of architecture, to help their local communities and to justify whatever public benefits the universities receive. Third, this approach could expose students to a wider range of experiences than they might get in a typical office, giving them client contact, management responsibility, and the like. While funding remains an issue, the idea of practice centers holds great promise, not the least of which is the potential to form an intermediary public institution between schools and practice, such as hospitals have become for physicians.

The medical profession found a singular system, the residency programs in hospitals, to help students become professionals. The architectural profession has several paths to achieve a similar end. Just as some of the architectural schools are more theory oriented, some more socially active, some more technical or practice oriented, so, too, will schools arrive at different solutions to the problem of preparing students for practice. Already, we have some work-study programs, a practice center established, and several schools talking about establishing teaching offices. Such diversity is just fine. Out of this experimentation, some ideas will falter, others succeed, and new ones are bound to emerge. In the present condition, with firms courting labor law or IRS violations, schools torn between serving the discipline and the profession, and students victimized by haphazard internships, one thing is clear: we cannot keep going as we are.

On a radio talk show once, the interviewer began by asking me, Is architecture ethical? The question caught me off guard. I had never asked myself and yet a talk-show host, speaking to a general audience, found the question of interest. I recall stumbling out something to the effect that architecture and ethics are connected in that both involve the relationships and responsibilities of people to each other. That question has continued to nag at me ever since, in part because I don't think the answer is as simple as I made it out to be on the radio.

Architecture, for example, has long been viewed as a branch of aesthetics rather than ethics. If anything, ethics has been thought of as applying to architects and not to architecture, to the actions of professionals, not the traits of buildings. Yet most people certainly talk as if architecture has an ethical component when we say that a building is good or bad, accommodating or mean, well-mannered or obtrusive. Our profession, however, has not attended enough to the connection between buildings and ethics, and that has gotten us in trouble.

The most obvious example of this has been modern urbanism. Architects and planners after World War II sold the idea of urban renewal, slum clearance, highway construction, and towers in parking lots as the result of a rational analysis of modern problems and as the most efficient application of modern technology. As such, this form of urbanism had the appearance of ethical neutrality and scientific inevitability. In reality, modern urbanism embraced a set of idealistic, Hegelian ethical propositions, including elevating the state over the individual, valuing progress over the past, and trusting a few visionaries (Hegel's world historical figures) to lead us into the future. The design professions may have portrayed urban renewal as ethically neutral, but the public seemed well aware of its ethical implications. Consider the rise, in the 1960s and 1970s, of the preservation movement, design review boards, and "not-in-my-backyard" sentiments. These were largely reactions, I believe, to the Hegelian ethics embedded in modern urbanism, which were rarely discussed by politicians or professionals, and which ran counter to other American ideals, such as individualism and egalitarianism.

Modernist architects were not alone in wanting to suppress the ethical component of what they did. Philosophers gave it credence. The reigning philosophy of the early decades of the century was called positivism, which held that we can only discuss that which we can quantifiably measure or rationally analyze. Since ethical—and aesthetic—questions are not easily quantified, positivists saw them as matters of opinion and personal preference, eliminating them from discussion. Positivism played into the hands of the professions, which sought legitimacy in the ability of their members to make (supposedly) objective evaluations of a problem and to find rational solutions to it. If ethics was discussed at all, it focused on professional practice rather than on the professional's actual work.

Positivism, however, raised a dilemma for architects, whose design decisions had always had, at least in the public's mind, a strong ethical component as well as an aesthetic one. Should architects embrace the subjectivity of ethics and aesthetics and risk losing the appearance of objectivity that had come to define professionalism, or should they embrace objectivity and risk losing connection to fundamental aspects of the art form? This is a question not yet settled, as is sometimes evident in the split between architectural educators and professionals.

One way to think our way out of this dilemma is to look at what positivism was reacting to in dismissing ethics and aesthetics. On the one hand, positivism represented a reaction to nineteenth-century idealism, with its advocacy of an absolute standard of the good and the beautiful. On the other hand, positivism rebelled against nineteenth-century utilitarianism, with its belief that the good or the beautiful could be determined as those that benefited the greatest number of people. By the end of the nineteenth century, the debate about ethics and aesthetics had become so polarized between an unattainable idealism and a calculating utilitarianism that one can understand the desire of positivists to throw the whole matter out. But that was not the only response to the situation.

An alternative arose in America in the form of pragmatism, which offered a reaction to idealism and utilitarianism that was, I believe, more amenable to architecture. Rather than dismiss ethics and aesthetics, pragmatism addressed these matters by looking at their consequences. A pragmatist would say that a building was good or beautiful if its full consequences were in themselves judged to be good or beautiful. There is, in other words, no intrinsic goodness or beauty in a building—no absolute standard against which to judge it—and no way to calculate the greatest good since the process of deciding the good or the beautiful is a never-ending process of interpretation and response. We can only make conditional judgments about ethical or aesthetic matters related to buildings. But judge we must, since buildings have consequences (they affect people), and no pretense of objectivity will change that fact.

The American reaction to nineteenth-century idealism and utilitarianism affected architecture deeply. At the same time that pragmatic thought was being developed by Charles Sanders Peirce, William James, and John Dewey, the architects Henry Hobson Richardson, Louis Sullivan, and Frank Lloyd Wright were developing a related response to the idealistic Classical architecture and to the utilitarian industrial buildings of their time. This parallel development in philosophy and architecture was not coincidental. The architecture of Richardson, Sullivan, and Wright was, in many ways, a concrete realization of pragmatism, the consequence of a philosophy that shaped the intellectual climate in which they worked.

Pragmatism was first formulated by the Boston philosopher Charles Sanders Peirce, who was born one year after the architect H. H. Richardson. Richardson, too, at one time lived and worked in Boston and, like Peirce, did his best work in a brief period from the late 1870s to the mid-1880s. Both Richardson, architecturally, and

Peirce, philosophically, formulated a new and quite similar way of dealing with European precedent. Richardson transformed the Romanesque architecture he visited while studying in France into an expression of the power and dynamism that had come to characterize late-nineteenth-century American society. Projects such as his Marshall Field Wholesale Store in Chicago provided a flexible and yet expressive framework for human activity, without becoming either a historical pastiche or an anonymous utilitarian structure.

Peirce also worked from European precedents, adapting them to uniquely American circumstances. He was influenced by Hegel, especially his idea that one can only understand something over time, and that every period has its own zeitgeist, its own way of interpreting what has come before. Rather than seeing things in rigidly Hegelian terms, where everything moves from a thesis and antithesis to a new synthesis, Peirce recognized in Hegel's thought a dynamic quality, well suited to the results-oriented Americans of his time. He shifted thinking away from judging things according to some ideal and toward evaluating things according to their actual consequences, that is, their effects over time.

Richardson died young, and Peirce never organized his thinking into a coherent system. The architect Louis Sullivan and the philosopher William James, became the interpreters of their ideas. They, too, had Boston connections: Sullivan was born there and James spent most of his professional life there. While they were further apart in age (James was fourteen years older than Sullivan), they both did their best work in a burst of creative energy in the 1890s through the first decade of the twentieth century.

Influenced by Richardson's effort in seeking an architectural expression for the dynamic quality of American culture, Sullivan tried to develop the principles behind such an effort and to write about them for a broad audience. The search for new and more dynamic architectural forms became linked in his mind to the openness and experimental nature of democracy. Through his work, with its open plans and broad gestures, Sullivan sought to express the pragmatic, democratic view that we must forever reevaluate what we consider to be good or true as new conditions arise.

James played a similar interpretive role for Peirce's ideas. Late in life, James wrote several essays that broadcast the ideas of pragmatism to a much larger audience than Peirce ever reached. Also, like Sullivan, James believed strongly in democratic action as a model for determining truth. Indeed, James constantly argued that we can never know the entire consequences of our actions or their full meaning. Thus we must believe and be willing to act without complete knowledge.

Sullivan and James did much to increase the awareness of this peculiarly American way of responding to European thought, although their contribution had its limits. Sullivan's architecture seemed, at times, too superficial, frequently a matter of placing ornamented facades on otherwise straightforward loft buildings. Likewise, James's description of pragmatism seemed, at times, too glib, when he equated the good with whatever works, sowing the seeds of a vulgar form of pragmatism that viewed the consequences of every action in the shortest term and in the narrowest economic sense.

It took another generation, that of Frank Lloyd Wright and John Dewey, to construct a more thoroughly integrated system in architecture and philosophy, respectively, and to articulate the broad social implications of the pragmatic approach. Richardson and Sullivan's pragmatic take on European precedent, for example, rarely addressed, as Wright's did, the urban scale on the one hand and the scale of dinnerware on the other. Nor were Richardson and Sullivan able to capture the attention of the public and to create architecture so all-encompassing, down to the smallest detail, as well as Wright did.

Dewey recognized that pragmatism, which for Peirce and James involved primarily individual judgment, served well as a social philosophy, as a way of judging social and governmental policy. Likewise, Dewey saw the power of pragmatism in addressing a wide range of issues, from education to ethics, language to logic. He communicated this in accessible prose, making him perhaps the last serious philosopher that the general public read, just as Wright became one of the last architects to have broad public name recognition.

Wright and Dewey became the leaders in their respective fields in America by the 1940s. However, World War II created a crisis for pragmatism, revealing the limits of that mode of thought. Although Wright pursued the social and urban implications of pragmatism, his emphasis on the individual and family unit in a world of private life and personal freedom seemed at odds with the collective solidarity needed during wartime. Dewey, too, seemed out of step during the war. His emphasis on judging the good in terms of its consequences proved inadequate to deciding what actions to take in a war in which the consequences were unknowable.

Wright and Dewey were as renowned after the war as they were before, but they lost their former intellectual leadership. The ideas of both were co-opted by others. Wright's agrarian vision became the model of suburban developers spacing identical houses across the land, while Dewey's social pragmatism devolved into a philosophy of the philistine, where ideas that did not have immediate practical utility were dismissed. The notion of judging things according to their consequences got turned around to mean that only things with known consequences would be considered. The good or beautiful became whatever worked, usually either from a functional or economic perspective.

This debased, reductive form of pragmatism has had a dampening effect on architecture perhaps more than other art forms because of our field's inevitable tie to utility. The other arts have sometimes been bracketed off as a castor oil of culture, harmless when taken in small doses. But architecture cannot be disconnected, and since World War II it has struggled under the misguided notion that the direct, natural, unornamented character of American architecture in the vein of Richardson, Sullivan, and Wright condones a minimal investment in anything other than the bare necessities in buildings. As every architect knows, the world is now full of "pragmatic" clients who seem to view almost any architectural exploration as a waste of time and money.

Pragmatism, in its original sense, offers architecture a way out of this dilemma. The so-called pragmatists of our time are generally concerned only with the immediate consequences of their actions: will a building meet market expectations right away or bring in a short-term profit? A true pragmatist would argue that the meaning and value of an action depends upon its consequences over time and that by attending only to immediate effects, we may in fact completely misjudge what we do.

Architects have a real, if rarely exploited, advantage: through postoccupancy evaluations and ongoing work for clients, we could counter the debased form of pragmatism by rigorously studying the effects of our decisions over extended periods of time, and communicating the lessons learned in a way that benefits the entire profession. When a client asks us to speed up the design process beyond reason or to switch to cheaper materials or to have no involvement in the construction phase, we should be armed with knowledge of the consequences of such actions. We should know the long-term effect of an unreasonably shortened design process, the long-term durability and maintenance cost of that cheaper material, or the long-term effect of excluding designers from the construction process. Likewise, we should have some sense of the effects of particular design decisions on people.

Why we have not armed ourselves with this knowledge is complicated. Clients usually won't pay for it and the profession has yet to find a way to fund this research collectively, as it should. Also, some architects seem to think that by examining the consequences of what we do, we will somehow destroy the "art" of architecture or leave the profession of architecture open to criticism. This only shows how far we have strayed from the pragmatism that offered so much promise for architecture earlier in the twentieth century, and how much we have misunderstood our own American architectural tradition. The work of Richardson, Sullivan, and Wright did not just represent an American architectural expression, as most of us have been taught. It also represented a particularly American form of pragmatism, where professionals would take full responsibility for the design of every aspect of the environment and for the consequences of those actions. We have instead reached a point where architects face ever-decreasing responsibility, and are protected in standard contracts from the consequences of almost everything that might go wrong in a project. This isn't pragmatism, at least as it was first conceived. It is, instead, what pragmatism has devolved into, a kind of antipragmatism that debilitates the profession.

Architecture is ethical because it has real consequences in the lives of people. And the ethics of being an architect involves knowing what those consequences are and taking responsibility for them. That is the promise that pragmatism originally held for architects, and it is the only defense we now have against what pragmatism has become.

In February 1988, *Progressive Architecture* magazine
published the results of a survey polling one thousand
randomly selected North American architects for their
opinion of professional ethics. The results were not
encouraging. Some 65 percent of those polled thought
that a significant number of their colleagues engaged in
some form of unethical behavior; 78 percent thought
that the code of ethics and professional conduct of the
American Institute of Architects was too weak to have
much of an influence over practitioners; and 90 percent
thought that the AIA would be reluctant to enforce the
code even if violations were brought to its attention.

Why such disillusionment with the behavior
of our colleagues and with the AIA's code of ethics and
its enforcement? I don't claim to have an answer to
such questions, but I thought that I might offer some
perspective as to why we have a code of ethics in the
first place, why it has not been as effective as we might
hope, and what we might do about it.

The author of that 1988 *P/A* article, John Morris Dixon, attributed the unethical behavior to the profession's being "engaged in intense competition, pressed for money, and tempted to please clients at any cost." Dixon also acknowledged that "the possibilities of self-policing in the profession are limited both by lack of agreement in some areas and by the government's restrictions on efforts that might affect competition."

If competitive pressures push architects toward unethical behavior today, they were also the cause of the very first discussions of ethics in the profession. As Henry Saylor writes in his history *The AIA's First Hundred Years*, competition was "perhaps the most disturbing factor in the relations of architect to architect and architect to potential client." As a result, in December 1909, the Institute wrote the first code of ethics, with the catchy title "Circular of Advice Relative to Principles of Professional Practice and the Canons of Ethics."

To our ear, some parts of that first code sound downright uptight. "It is improper," it said, "to (1.) engage in building; (2.) guarantee an estimate; (3.) accept payment from anyone other than a client; (4.) to pay for advertising; (5.) to take any part in a competition not approved by the AIA." Other parts of that first code, however, sound all too familiar, such as calling it unethical "(9.) to injure falsely or maliciously the reputation of a fellow practitioner; (10.) to undertake work in which there is an unsettled claim; (11.) to attempt to supplant another architect already engaged."

The biggest changes in the code of ethics from 1909 to this day have been the disappearance of prohibitions against competition and the increased use of broader ethical concepts, such as honesty, fairness, dignity, and integrity. These changes have made the code more safe; even the Justice Department cannot dispute the advocating of honesty or fairness. But, as the *P/A* reader poll suggests, such terms may have made the code so broad as to be ineffectual. The AIA's own Office of the General Counsel offers evidence of that in its advisory opinions, which it writes in response to specific ethical dilemmas that members face, such as uncompensated design services, referral fees, endorsements, gender discrimination, use of another architect's drawings, and so on. Those opinions are useful and interesting to read. They highlight, however, the deficiencies of the code, whose broad statements seem contrary to the specificity and concreteness that ethics demands.

Ethics arises out of a dilemma, a situation in which right and wrong are not entirely clear, and codes of ethics are an attempt to prevent such dilemmas from recurring by developing principles to guide our behavior. The question is why, in 1909, did this occur in architecture? What dilemmas did the profession face that prompted the writing of the first code? And why, some fifty years after the founding of the Institute, did members see a need to regulate the behavior of their colleagues?

The answer to those questions lies, in part, in a shift that occurred in the profession in the latter part of the nineteenth century away from a vernacular, apprentice form of education to the competition-based French system of education associated with the École des Beaux-Arts. While that system is still very much with us and has been the source of much good in the profession, its transplantation to these shores created some enormous conflicts for architects.

In France, competitions largely occurred for governmental projects within a political system that was highly centralized and regulated. When that same system was imported here, however, our less regulated free-market system and less centralized government began to use competitions differently from what was done in France. As Saylor observes, competitions became an opportunity for exploitation by unscrupulous clients and a major source of unethical behavior on the part of some architects.

Ironically, while the number of competitions and the amount of corruption associated with them increased, architects were simultaneously attempting to control competition through professionalization. Like other professions, we sought to have the various states grant us a monopoly over our area of practice through licensure in exchange for the greater good that comes from our advancing knowledge and attending to public health and safety needs. Other professions such as law and medicine have managed, until relatively recently, to limit competitive pressures on their fees in the marketplace. But unlike those others, the architectural profession has been of two minds about competitions, making a code of ethics almost inevitable for us. If we couldn't control the behavior of clients in the system we ourselves had helped establish, we could at least try to control the behavior of our colleagues— with mixed results, as the *P/A* survey shows.

The mixed results are, in some respects, inherent in the very idea of a written code of ethics. First, codifying ethical behavior in a set of principles is extremely difficult. Such principles either become so prescriptive that they run afoul, at least in this country, of our government-enforced free-market system, or so broad that they become platitudes that few can argue with and everyone can ignore. Second, ethics has a dynamic quality that can get lost in the codifying. Ethical dilemmas are ever changing and so difficult to address with codified standards. Indeed, the frequency with which the AIA has rewritten its code of ethics demonstrates the difficulty of trying to reduce behavior that is almost infinitely varied to relatively few principles.

Experiencing similar difficulties, other professions have begun to see ethics not just as the subject for a written code, but as the basis for an ongoing conversation about what constitutes good behavior or the right decision under particular conditions. Legal ethics and, most notably, medical ethics have become major areas of debate and discussion in those fields, with whole conferences and entire journals devoted to the subjects.

The architectural profession, I believe, needs to begin its own ongoing ethical discourse; at the least, symposia addressing the subject should be a regular feature of professional conferences. Like our colleagues in other professions, however, we face real obstacles to engaging in that conversation because of the desiccated state of modern ethics. "The resources of most modern moral philosophy," writes the philosopher Bernard Williams, "are not well adjusted to the modern world." Ethics, he continues, "is too far removed, as Hegel first said it was, from social and historical reality and from any concrete sense of a particular ethical life.... It is not a paradox that in these very new circumstances very old philosophies may have more to offer than moderately new ones."

Like Williams, I believe that some "very old philosophies" can help us understand and resolve many of today's ethical dilemmas. To show how and why that is so, I will use four classical theories of ethics as a framework within which we might begin a conversation about some of the ethical issues we face as a profession.

Before I take up those questions, let me provide a bit of the ethical context surrounding the AIA's 1909 code. It emerged at a time when ethics was undergoing a modernist revolution of sorts, set off by the work of the German philosopher Friedrich Nietzsche and the English philosopher G. E. Moore. In books such as *The Will to Power*, published in 1901, Nietzsche argued that the dominant Christian ethics of his day weakened Western cultures in the Darwinian struggle for supremacy. Turning traditional ethics on its head, Nietzsche elevated the values of the individual will and the power of the strong over the weak, the very things that moral philosophy had for so long sought to curb.

In a more mild-mannered but no less radical move, G. E. Moore in his 1903 book *Principia Ethica* argued that the "good" is a simple, unanalyzable property that we can know through intuition, but cannot define. Moore and his students, such as Bertrand Russell, succeeded in removing ethics as a subject about which we have anything to say.

I don't mean to suggest that the AIA's code of ethics was a direct result of these books. I doubt that more than a handful of architects were even aware of Nietzsche or Moore at the time. But I think that, as so often happens in the history of thought, these philosophies articulated a point of view that had already become relatively widespread; the speed with which Nietzsche and Moore's ideas were embraced indicates a readiness on the part of many people for them.

Needed: A Conversation about Ethics

By dismissing most of the ethical past and envisioning an ethical future of personal intuition and individual will, Nietzsche and Moore mark a shift in Western ethics. No longer could we assume that people would obey the traditional standards and expectations of behavior, the so-called gentlemen's agreements upon which much of eighteenth- and nineteenth-century society relied. In response, more explicit and more legalistic forms of regulating behavior arose in the early twentieth century. Codes of ethics, along with building and zoning codes, were established during the same era to control by external means the restraints that in previous periods had been internalized in most individuals and enforced through more informal means such as tradition and peer pressure. The AIA's code of ethics, in other words, might be seen as a response to and a product of modernism. The discourse about ethics that has begun to emerge in recent years among the professions might be seen as a modernist critique, an effort to recover guidance for the future from the ethical debates of the past.

Let's begin at the traditional starting point of Western ethics, with Plato. He argued that unethical behavior stemmed from a lack of knowledge or, put another way, that people would act ethically if they understood the full consequences of not doing so. This is admittedly an optimistic and idealistic view; Plato assumes that unethical behavior arises from ignorance rather than, say, evil. His position, which has been extremely influential over the past 2,300 years, underlies a number of the standards and rules of conduct in the AIA's code of ethics.

For example, the opening line of the code states that members should "strive to improve their professional knowledge and skill," echoing the Platonic belief that ethical behavior derives from education and self-improvement. At the same time, Plato believed that an absolute "good" exists for every situation and that we can arrive at it through continual questioning, echoed in the code's urging members to "continually seek to raise the standards of aesthetic excellence, architectural education, research, training, and practice."

Plato's ethics works best when the consequences of actions are clear. For example, when the AIA's code of ethics calls for members to "uphold the law in the conduct of their professional activities," the consequences of not doing so are obvious. The law becomes, if not the absolute good, at least that which we should absolutely avoid breaking. Indeed, the code has more of a legal tone than it does an ethical one, using such legalistic terms as human rights, discrimination, fraud, and conflict of interest. That no doubt reflects the Office of General Counsel's involvement in helping draft the AIA code. It also shows, however, how much ethics itself has been reduced to and defined as legal behavior rather than in a traditional sense of the "good." The AIA's code of ethics doesn't even use the word "good," perhaps because of the difficulty of defining it in a court of law, even though the definition of that word lies at the very heart of ethical discourse.

Back to Plato. His ethics, for all of its insight, fails us when the consequences of behavior lack clarity. In the *P/A* survey, for example, readers split over whether or not certain actions were unethical, such as paying recent graduates exceptionally low wages in exchange for work experience. Some 35 percent thought it was unethical; 65 percent thought not. Plato's ethics offers relatively little guidance here, in part because the consequences of paying low wages are not obvious. It clearly affects the employees, who may not make enough to live on, but what if they accept the low wages as a trade-off for desired experience? Low wages also affect the bottom line and reputation of the firm, in opposite ways, but how much weight do we place on one over the other? Also, if such a practice became common enough, it would negatively affect the image of the profession, which it already has to some extent. But is that enough to overcome the practice's other benefits?

Such questions are the sort that a discourse about ethics in the profession should take up. They lie beyond the generalities of the written code, which simply states that "members should provide their associates and employees with a suitable working environment, compensate them fairly, and facilitate their professional development." Arriving at a consensus about such dilemmas demands an ongoing conversation, because only then will we come to know their full meaning and their real consequences.

One of the strongest critics of Plato's ethics was his student Aristotle, who believed that more than one right course of action existed for a given situation, and that we had to have a way of judging the good without waiting for full knowledge of its consequences, which often is impossible, anyway. Ethics, for Aristotle, had as its goal a happy life, which he believed was best achieved through the moderation of extremes. The ethical person, for instance, exhibits a proper pride as the mean between empty vanity and undue humility or a liberality with money as the mean between prodigality and meanness.

The AIA's code of ethics has many passages that echo that Aristotelian moderation. In the standard that urges members to "serve their clients in a timely and competent manner," timely could be said to represent the mean between, say, super-fast-tracking and outright sloth. But what about competence? Is it really the mean between incompetence and overcompetence? Imagine telling your client that you offer a moderate amount of competence, but not too much.

If Aristotle's ethics encounters difficulties dealing with concepts that don't lend themselves to the moderation of extremes, so, too, does his ethics fall short when dealing with such absolutes as the law. Take the rule in the AIA code that says "members shall not ... knowingly violate the law." Violating the law in moderation—as the mean between being law abiding and, say, a major criminal—is not an ethical option.

Still, Aristotle's ideas can contribute to a discourse about ethics in the profession. A number of ethical dilemmas that can occur in the course of architectural practice, such as accepting gifts from contractors and building product manufacturers or moonlighting while employed in a firm, could benefit from an Aristotelian analysis. Do all gifts or all moonlighting count as unethical, or should the size of the gift or the amount of moonlighting affect our view? Is occasional moonlighting that does not affect an employee's performance the same as someone working two full-time jobs? Is a modest gift given as a token of appreciation, with more sentimental than monetary value, the same as one given to influence a decision?

The AIA code implies a difference when it says, for example, that "Members shall neither offer nor make any payment or gift to a public official with the intent of influencing the official's judgment." Yet how can we measure someone's intent or base an enforceable code upon it? Such are the questions that Aristotle's ethics can help us sort out.

Needed: A Conversation about Ethics

The "old philosophies" of the Romans also offer some guidance in dealing with our ethical dilemmas as a profession. For example, stoic thinkers such as Epictetus or the Roman emperor Marcus Aurelius thought that unethical actions occur when people are overly influenced by and dependent upon external circumstances. Ethical behavior, they believed, stems from individuals becoming indifferent to outside influence and taking responsibility for only that which the individual can control.

Those ideas find their way into the AIA code in statements such as "Members shall not sign or seal drawings, specifications, reports, or other professional work for which they do not have responsible control," or "Members should avoid conflict of interest in their professional practices." Such stress on the avoidance of responsibility or conflict recalls the stoic goal of achieving a calm indifference as the route to a good life.

The difficulty here is that professionals can rarely afford to be indifferent, even if we'd like to. As most architects learn at some point in their careers, denying responsibility for actions beyond our control does not mean that we will not get sued. Nor does the denial of responsibility jibe with the notion of the professional as a person prepared to take knowledgeable risk, or with our own self-image as a profession concerned about public issues. Can anyone engaged in this most social of the arts afford to withdraw into a stoic calm?

There is a reason, though, why we hear the echo of stoicism not only in the AIA's code of ethics, but in the AIA's standard contracts, which over the years have sought to relieve architects of responsibility and with it, some claim, an adequate reward for our effort. The connection between stoicism and American law runs deep. As the legal theorist W. Friedmann writes, "The stoics first developed a coherent legal philosophy based upon the individual as a reasonable being ... [with] inalienable rights," which, in turn, has been the intellectual basis of much American jurisprudence. Attorneys—like good stoics—seem constitutionally driven, both literally and figuratively, to insulate us from risk. Any discourse on ethics in the profession must address this issue. We need to decide whether we want our code of ethics to reflect our values or those of our lawyers.

Another useful ethical position that we inherited from the Romans is hedonism. The inverse of the stoic's avoidance of pain, the hedonist seeks pleasure as the sole good. And, in part because so much of our ethical codes have derived from stoicism, hedonism seems like the very thing we write such codes to guard against. After all, the unethical behavior of professionals often involves the taking advantage of a person or a situation for personal gain or pleasure.

The notion of pleasure that hedonism originally propounded, however, was not at all inconsistent with a code of ethics such as the AIA's. The Roman philosopher, Epicurus, held that the greatest pleasures of life are knowledge and the mutual respect of friends. So, when the AIA's code urges members to "recognize and respect the professional contributions of their employees, employers, professional colleagues, and business associates," it has a distinctly Epicurean sound.

Yet, the *P/A* survey suggests that the unethical treatment of employees and colleagues ranks among the most common violations. Respondents listed "putting one's seal on drawings one has not supervised" as one of the most frequent abuses, followed by such actions as "accepting full credit for work that others collaborated on" or "hiring/keeping employees with false promises of advancement."

Why the frequency of this behavior? It may stem, in part, from the very nature of architectural practice, which seems structured to promote the pleasure of a few over the many. The division of labor and structure of relationships in all but the smallest architectural offices set up situations in which partners get credit for the work of employees or sign drawings others have produced.

With such an ethical dilemma, a modified version of hedonism—utilitarianism—might be of some use. The nineteenth-century thinkers Jeremy Bentham and John Stuart Mill proposed the principle of utility as a way of overcoming the problem of equating hedonism with personal pleasure and power. Instead, they argued, we must look to what produces the greatest happiness or pleasure for the greatest number of people.

Although the principle of utility may now be as misunderstood as hedonism, it does at least give us a way of evaluating the effects of exploiting employees or misrepresenting responsibility in an office. An action that fails the test of utility—that does not extend the greatest happiness or satisfaction to the greatest number of people—fails for everyone, the perpetrator of the action as well as its recipients. A selfish hedonism literally has no utility, no use especially in a setting such as an architectural office where the interdependence of employees and employer makes the happiness of the greatest number crucial to the ability of the firm to perform.

At this point, you might be wondering what good all of this talk about ethics is if it can't be enforced. Remember that 90 percent of those who responded to the *P/A* poll thought that the code of ethics would not be enforced even if violations were brought to the attention of the AIA.

There are a couple of ways to think about enforcement, one that is more common and another that is more effective. The more common approach says that a violation of the code of ethics can lead to the suspension of membership in the AIA or, depending upon the violation, prosecution under the law. This echoes the ethical position of the eighteenth-century thinker Immanuel Kant, who argued that we have a duty as members of a society to obey its ethical obligations and that society, in turn, has an absolute right to punish us for our lapses in this duty. He acknowledged that there might be situations that demanded we act according to our conscience, even if it goes against a societal practice, and he gave us a few rules to go by in this: "act as if every action were to become a universal law" and "treat every person as an end, rather than as a means to some other end." You hear these precepts in such passages in the AIA code as "members shall not engage in conduct involving fraud or wanton disregard of the rights of others."

The difficulties you run into with Kant's formalism, and with depending upon the threat of punishment as the basis for enforcing the code of ethics, involve situations in which there is a conflict between duties. One example relates to the conflict in the AIA code between the standard that says that "members should uphold the law in the conduct of their professional activities," and the one that says that "members should safeguard the trust placed in them by their clients."

It may happen that one aspect of the law, as written, appears to violate another, as was true in a recent first amendment case involving the Mall of America in Bloomington, Minnesota. Because the Mall is privately owned and so able, according to property law, to determine the speech and behavior of those who enter, its owners created a place for free speech outside, in the middle of a traffic island. The state courts, however, decided that this violated the first amendment of Minnesota's constitution, which not only protects free speech but also prohibits any physical act that would prevent it (a decision that was subsequently overturned upon appeal). Which law does the architect follow in such a case? What happens when the client's wishes meet one interpretation of the law and violate another? And how can an organization such as the AIA punish violators of a code when the ethical issues underlying the code are so variable in interpretation?

The second, less common, and possibly more effective way of enforcing ethical behavior draws from the work of the twentieth-century thinker John Dewey. In some ways, Dewey's ethical position echoes that of Plato in the sense that both believed that we can judge right or wrong by informing ourselves of the full consequences of an action. Dewey and Plato part ways, however, where Plato held that there is a single, universal right action for every ethical dilemma, which, if we don't see, simply means that we are uninformed. Dewey instead realized that notions of right and wrong change over time and from one culture to another.

The advisory opinions from the AIA's general counsel are full of Dewey's consequentialist thinking. One example deals with an architect who took a referral fee from a contractor. "The acceptance of a referral fee from the person that the architect recommended affects the interest of persons other than the architect and the contractor," the opinion states, going on to say that it affects the building owner and potentially the public at large.

The difficulty that has always been raised with Dewey's approach is the same as the criticism leveled at Plato: how does one know what are the full consequences of an action? How can one put off making ethical judgments until one has all the information? As an individual, you can't. But you can as part of an organization and as a profession, which is precisely what the medical profession is engaged in. Through conversation, debate, and documentation, it is slowly building knowledge of the consequences of one medical decision versus another, and is developing ethical principles based on that knowledge.

As I said, the architectural profession needs to do the same, if for no other reason than to be able to enforce our own code of ethics. Enforcement here would not be through punishment, but through the ability to inform those who would act unethically—employers who think they don't have to pay employees, clients who think they can ask for free services, architects who think they can slander competitors—of the real, negative consequences of such behavior. Ethics, in the end, defines what we, as a community and a society, agree is in our collective best interest. It is through our acting as a community, informing each other of the consequences of actions and conversing about what consequences we judge to be good or bad, that we may begin to achieve the ethical behavior we aspire to.

There will undoubtedly remain architects who are skeptical about any sort of ethical discussion. Whether conscious of it or not, they may adhere to the ethical naturalism of Nietzsche, which pits one person against another in a survival of the fittest, or in the ethical realism of G. E. Moore, for whom any attempt at defining the ethical good is impossible. The problem such views pose for architecture is that they undermine our discipline in particular. Ethics looks at not only what constitutes good behavior, but what constitutes the good life, and both are intimately connected to the making of architecture. I do not mean to suggest that one must be a good person to make good architecture; history has long ago relieved us of that illusion. Rather, I want to argue that all good architecture puts forward a proposition, whether the designer is aware of it or not, about the good life, about how we should live and what we should live for. A sustained discourse about ethics, in other words, would help us to create not only a better profession, but better architecture, and that is a good we all share.

Index

A

Aesop, 84–89
Alexander, Christopher, 59
Alpha diversity, 20–22
American Institute of
 Architects, 8, 36, 95–96,
 133–149
Archilochus, 79, 84
Aristotle, 79, 141–142
Arts and Crafts, 71–72

B

Bacon, Francis, 14–15,
 16–17, 55–56
Barrett, William, 107
Bentham, Jeremy, 145
Berlin, Isaiah, 13, 14,
 79–80
Beta diversity, 22–24
Boyer, Ernest, 68
Broadacre City, 17, 66
Brown, Denise Scott, 82
Brownfield sites, 23
Burnham, Daniel, 15–16,
 25, 84
Burroughs, William, 71

C

Carnegie Foundation
 for the Advancement of
 Teaching, 68
Ceaușescu, Nicholae, 16
Center for Public
 Architecture, 121
City Beautiful, 15–16
Classicism, 60, 61, 126
Clausen, Christopher, 13,
 68, 69
Commodification, 39–45,
 49, 112

D

Dante, 79
Darwin, Charles, 2, 138
Derrida, Jacques, 25
Descartes, René, 14,
 15–16, 21
Dewey, John, 17, 126, 129,
 130, 147–148
Dillard, Annie, 71
Diversity, 20–25
Dixon, John Morris, 134
Duany, Plater-Zyberk, 20
Duban, 69

Index

Steiner, George, 105–106, 110
Stirling, James, 56
Stoicism, 145–146
Sullivan, Louis, 126–130

T
Taylor, Frederick, 55
Teaching office, 120–121
Temporal diversity, 24–25
Terry, Quinlan, 60–61
Theory, critical, 112
Thomas, Lewis, 115
Thoreau, Henry David, 71
Tolstoy, Leo, 79–80, 83

U
UCLA, 118
Universities, 3–4, 5, 7–11, 29, 36,
    47–48, 68, 91–92, 105–106,
    115–122
University of Cincinnati, 118
Urban Innovations Group,
    119–120
Urbanism, 21, 124
Utilitarianism, 125, 126, 145
Utopias, 13, 14–18, 25

V
Vaihinger, Hans, 53, 62, 63
Van Alen Institute, 121
Venturi, Robert, 82–83
Viollet-le-Duc, Eugène-Emanuel, 69
Virtual firms, 4–5, 96, 120
Voltaire, 18

W
Ware, William, 69
Watkin, David, 70
Webb, Philip, 80
Williams, Bernard, 137
Wilson, William Julius, 20
Wittgenstein, Ludwig, 104, 106
Wittkower, Rudolf, 70
Wölfflin, Heinrich, 70
Work-study programs, 118–119
Wren, Christopher, 80
Wright, Frank Lloyd, 17, 25, 43,
    57, 60, 62, 66, 80, 86, 117,
    126, 129–130, 131

Y
Yale University, 9

Z
Zanten, David van, 69–70
Zoar, Ohio, 14

THOMAS R. FISHER is dean of the College of Architecture and Landscape Architecture at the University of Minnesota, coeditor of *Architectural Research Quarterly*, and former editorial director of *Progressive Architecture*. His essays have appeared in *Design Quarterly*, *Architectural Record*, and other leading journals.